Contents

Foreword

You know the kids are crazy about it. Throw them a soccer ball (better yet, kick it to them) and suddenly they're like kittens with catnip. They get carried away by the flow of the game. They get totally absorbed, totally engrossed, totally fascinated.

And you know the game does something for you too. When the kids get that excited, you get excited with them. Soccer has such a magnetic appeal that you can't help getting carried away by it.

What you don't know is how you get so deeply involved so quickly. The local youth league was desperately in need of coaches. They asked you a question you couldn't refuse: "Will you help out?"

So suddenly you're the coach of a young and eager team, and you have to prepare them for league competition. What you want to know is, "Who's going to help *me* out?"

You grew up on football, basketball, and baseball. You know next to nothing about soccer. Somehow you've got to take a crash course in the basic skills and how to use them in the game. On top of that, you've got to learn how to coach all of this. That's where Bobby Moffat and his book come into the picture.

The Basic Soccer Guide is first and foremost a practical book. Part Two sets firm foundations in the basic skills. Part Three builds a wider knowledge of the game on that foundation. The Appendix includes the laws of the game, a special section on the offside rule, a soccer glossary, and a concluding essay on the past, present, and future of the game.

If you're involved in youth soccer, you'll see immediately that Bobby's book talks directly to your needs.

"Who's going to help *me* out?" Bobby Moffat, that's who.

by Ian Jackson, Soccer World Editor

Meet Bobby Moffat

When Bobby let me read the first draft of *The Basic Soccer Guide,* I knew he'd have no trouble finding a publisher. I knew not only because of the quality of the book but also because of Bobby's enthusiasm and competence in the other ventures he has already pursued.

You probably already know of Bobby's stellar performance in the North American Soccer League as a player for the Dallas Tornado. In his nine years with the Tornado he played every position except goalkeeper. What you may not know is that he is just as versatile off the field as on.

His syndicated television show, *Soccer Locker,* ran for three years; and his skill in handling clinics puts him in ever-increasing demand. When I began reading his book, I was eager to see if he had writing talent as well as solid soccer expertise. He does, without a doubt. I think his book is excellent.

It is completely free from the "one-upmanship" I find in so many coaching books. Many authors seem more interested in mystifying than clarifying, perhaps because they hope this will give the impression that they know more than they do. Bobby steers clear of this. He's concerned with helping beginners, not with impressing people about his insight into the more esoteric aspects of the game. We've needed a book like this for a long time, and we'll need it for many years to come.

by Kyle Rote, Jr.

PART ONE

HOW TO USE THE GUIDE

Explanations of the basic skills

The explanations of the basic skills are written for beginners—whether they be coaches or players. A coach can simply explain the skills to his players, using the photographs in the book to make everything clear. If the coach himself learns the basic skills in the manner presented in the book, it will help him understand his players' problems better.

Exercises

Immediately following the explanation of each basic skill are skill practice exercises. Read the instructions carefully.

Requirements for exercises

The description of each exercise is preceded by a brief list of what you need to set up the practice—how to arrange the players, how many balls you need, etc. The book supplies the exercises, you supply the boys, the balls (the more the better), and the field.

Levels of Difficulty

Each exercise is marked as Level one, two, or three. Level one is really basic, Level two is a little more advanced, Level three is the most advanced in the book.

When to Advance

Move your players on to a more advanced practice only when they have progressed sufficiently to warrant it. Don't rush them, nurse them along. Lay the basic foundations securely. Bad habits become harder and harder to correct.

Select what you want

You don't have to use all the skill practice exercises. Pick the ones that fill your needs and pass over the others. Whichever exercises you use, however, proceed carefully and according to the Level one, two, three gradations.

If you are coaching for the first time, you will probably want to try all the exercises. A more experienced coach will have enough background to pick and choose. He understands a little better what he needs. He might start with the Level two exercises he feels can be particularly helpful to his team.

The need for a good service

A practice can only be as good as the service. If a player is practicing controlling the ball with his thigh, the ball has to be thrown to his thigh. He can't work on thigh control if the ball is thrown to his feet. A reliable service takes you half way towards having a good practice.

Read Left for Right

The explanations of the basic skills are written as if for right footed players only. The photographs illustrating the skills show the same bias. Left footed players need not despair. When reading the explanations and looking at the photographs, simply exchange "left" for "right" and vice versa.

Boys and Girls

There are a large number of girls playing soccer, and the numbers are rapidly growing. For simplicity, I have referred to players as "boys" throughout the book. Girls should not worry about this—just read "girls" for "boys."

Using the Line Method

When you see (Line method) beside an Exercise it signifies that the line method can be used. The line method is designed to avoid congestion and overlapping on basic practices when your boys are divided into pairs with a ball for each pair.

Look at the diagram. As you can see, the group is divided into two lines, facing each other. Each boy faces his partner on the opposite line; for instance, boy 2 is facing boy 2. If you decide to use this method, the distance between the two lines will be the same as the distance given under requirements, as the boys will be doing exactly the same exercise.

Always try to keep five yards between boys on the same line. This leaves a margin for error and gives your boys room to maneuver.

Try to maintain these lines. If a boy leaves his place on the line make sure he rejoins it at virtually the same spot. This may seem rather regimental, but you'll soon find it is necessary if you are to obtain the maximum from your practices. It helps to stop the confusion of boys and balls flying in all directions.

Walk around the outside of your group as they are practicing. By doing this you can see all of your group at a glance, and stop to give individual coaching where needed.

If you have an uneven number of players, form a triangle with three of the boys (assuming a ball per pair), or practice with the extra boy yourself, or have an assistant practice with him.

The Line Method

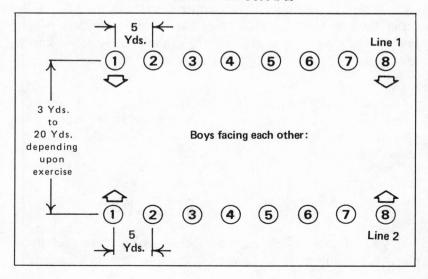

Tips for Better Coaching

● *Praise.* Be sure to praise and encourage the boys on your team. Remember, they are playing for enjoyment.

● *Both Feet.* Encourage your boys to use their weak foot as well as their good foot. Build up the habit of using both feet. It will pay dividends.

● *Compact.* When your boys are practicing basic skills try to keep them as compact as possible, without cramping the practice, so that you can be heard by the entire group when you want to make a point. (See line method, opposite page.)

● *Attention.* When talking to your boys demand their complete attention. Don't let anyone bounce a ball while you are talking and don't do it yourself. When you are talking to your group and they are sitting down, face them away from the sun and in the quietest spot you can find. Distractions ruin concentration. Remember that a young boy's attention span can be very limited.

● *Demonstrate.* When instructing your boys try, if at all possible, to demonstrate the skills you want them to perform. If you can't demonstrate, find a boy on your team with the skill to do it for you.

● *Improvise.* Coaches have to learn to improvise. You may turn up to practice on a field and find a game in progress. If this happens, you'll have to find some other piece of land, put down coats or whatever for goals and hold your practice. When using the exercises in this book, you may not have enough balls to go round one per pair. Improvise, while still trying to retain the essence of the exercise.

● *Calling.* Players can help teammates on the field by intelligent shouting. For instance, if an unmarked player is controlling the ball a good shout to him would be "Time". This means he has time to control the ball and then look up at the developing play. If the same player were tightly marked an intelligent shout would be "Man on." Encourage your boys to call to each other, as it can greatly contribute to your team's performance.

• *See games.* I recommend that the novice coach see as many soccer games as possible. At these games he can get an idea of the shape of soccer and learn a great deal just by watching. I suggest the coach take his entire team to see a professional game. This can be a great help in motivating your boys. It will show them what standards can be achieved.

• *Conditioned reflexes.* In coaching we try to instill certain reflexes or habits into players so that they will automatically use them in games. The formation of good habits, like watching the ball and using both feet, should start at a very basic stage. If you continually remind your players about good habits, they will automatically begin to adopt them. You can then build from this good base.

• *Move up defense.* As soon as the ball is cleared from the immediate danger area, move your defense up in front of the attackers, no further than the half-way line, so as to put the attackers into offside positions. (Set Play 2, page 91). This tactic confuses forwards at first, but after a while one may decide to go it alone and take on an outcoming defense which is square or flat. Crowd him, make him pass the ball. Remember, he cannot be offside if he dribbles the ball through by himself.

• *Coaching sessions.* Always attempt to make your practices as interesting and as well balanced as possible. I recommend that you divide your practice sessions into three general activity periods: Ten minutes of warm-ups—ball skills, team competitions (dribbling around a stake) etc.; thirty minutes of coaching exercises (This could be two 15-minute or three 10-minute periods); 20-minute scrimmage game.

• *A tip for your defenders.* When in doubt, kick it out. If a defender is unsure of the play and is being hustled, he should play the ball away. This is a wise move. A defender's trying to manuever a ball out of a tight situation, especially near his goal, could lead to his losing the ball and his team losing a goal.

• *A tip for your forwards.* Any time you are inside the penalty area and you have an opportunity to shoot, with a reasonable chance of success, don't hesitate. Shoot. The sooner the better. Don't give the goalkeeper time to prepare and set himself for a save.

• *Another tip for your forwards.* Follow the ball. This might seem obvious to you, but as it cannot be stressed enough I am mentioning it early. Stress this point to your forwards before every shooting practice and every game whether it is an important competition or a casual scrimmage.

Dennis Law, a Scotsman who has recently retired from playing in the English first division, is one of the most prolific goal-scorers of all time. He has scored many unforgettable goals. Around half of his goals, however, came from knock-downs and rebounds which he had followed-up. When the ball went into his opponents' goal-mouth, Dennis was always lurking around looking for an opportunity to score a simple looking goal. The simplest looking things are often the hardest to achieve. Dennis timed his runs to coincide with the drop of the ball. To be there too soon or too late is no good. One has to be there at the exact time. So stress following-up to your boys, not only on their own shots, but on their teammates' shots as well.

• *Wall practice.* Soccer can be enjoyed in its entirety or in part. A boy might have a ball but no one to play with. He can have fun juggling the ball or kicking, heading, or throwing it against a wall (preferably a wall without windows in it).

Many soccer skills can be practiced in this way—controlling the ball, first time passing, etc. Continually heading the ball against the wall is a good practice for getting a sense of rhythm. Goalkeepers can throw or kick the ball against the wall and catch the rebounds. A goal can be outlined for shooting practice, and circles can be drawn in the goal for accuracy kicking. There are many alternatives. You can work out a few for yourself. The ball very seldom comes to you exactly the way you want it to. You have to adjust to the rebounds off the wall.

• *Meet the ball.* Valuable seconds and good positions are wasted in waiting for the ball. Stress meeting the ball, whenever possible. A good line to use is "Don't wait for it, meet it."

• *Tether balls and Balloons.* A tether ball or a balloon can be a great help in learning the kicking action. A tether ball has a small tab of leather through which a rope can be threaded. By holding on to the rope, a player can practice repeated kicks on the dangling ball. A coach can hold the rope and run his team through kicking practice in quick succession so that each boy has to adjust very quickly to the ball. The tether ball can also be used to practice heading and trapping. It can be used in a wide variety of skill practices.

Kicking a balloon may sound like a strange practice for soccer. However, it can be useful in the early stages of learning because it gives the players time to adjust to a moving object. Once having succeeded with a balloon, beginners can quickly learn how to adjust to a faster moving soccer ball. Kick through the balloon for the greatest benefit.

● *Tennis Ball.* Juggling a tennis ball is a great exercise for skill and coordination and will undoubtedly increase a player's skill level.

The Coach's Responsibility

The coach is in charge of the team. I suggest he find one other person to assist him, at least to begin with. Two heads are better than one.

The coach decides who plays in what position, and for how long, the latter depending upon local substitution rules. He also decides upon practices and, eventually, tactics. He gives his time for practices and games so he has a right to enjoy a measure of success. This means he needs to organize. Organization of practices is a long step towards organization on the field.

Discipline is important. Make sure that your boys understand exactly what you expect from them right from the very beginning.

Be punctual. This is a form of discipline. If the coach is continually late, his boys will begin to arrive late too. Suggest that your boys arrive at the field 10 minutes before the scheduled start of each practice session.

The coach is in charge of boys of impressionable ages. His job is to teach, guide, and help them. He should be aware of these responsibilities.

In my opinion, a coach should openly criticize a boy only in extreme cases. It is better always to praise and encourage. I have had good results from praise and bad results from criticism. When a boy makes a mistake which you want to point out, speak to him in a quiet way or take him to one side. Boys appreciate this approach.

A coach should earn respect. Respect your boys and work hard for them and they will respect you.

PART TWO

LEARN THE BASIC SKILLS

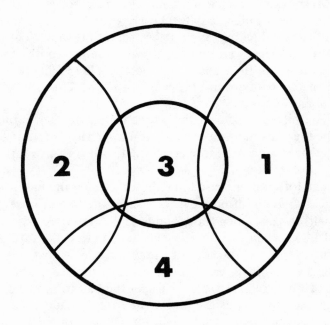

Where to Kick the Ball

Look at the diagram. It shows the part of the ball facing the kicker as he prepares to kick it. The ball is numbered. Each

number covers an area. If the kicker kicks straight through the
numbers the ball will go—
1. To the left.
2. To the Right.
3. Straight ahead. The ball will keep fairly low or travel
   along the ground. This is the area which is connected
   with by the kicker for accuracy kicking and the inside
   of the foot pass.
4. Straight ahead. The ball will rise. This is the area which
   is connected with by the kicker for the lofted pass.

Kicking with the Instep

Most Americans, when first kicking a soccer ball, kick it
with the toes. This is a natural carry-over from American football. But toe kicking, even at best, is inaccurate. That's why
soccer-style kickers are so popular with the pro football teams—
they score more field goals. In soccer-style kicking we wrap as
much of our foot around the ball as we can. This is how we get
control and accuracy.

The instep kick uses the whole top of the foot rather than
just the toe. The method of execution is slightly different depending on whether we are more concerned with getting a lofted pass
or an accurate kick.

The lofted pass is used mainly for kicking the ball over long
distances. With a lofted pass, there is less danger of interception
than with a pass along the ground. It is often used when taking
a goal kick, when the kicker needs height (to make sure the ball
isn't intercepted at the edge of the penalty area), distance (to get
the ball away from his goal), and accuracy (to place the ball within
reach of his players). In order to get the ball to rise, the trick is
to lean back slightly as the top of the foot contacts the ball.

To get more accuracy than is possible with the lofted pass,
keep your head and knee over the ball on contact, and flex the
ankle more (heel up, toe down). This helps keep the ball
low. It is a good kick to use on small and closely guarded targets,
such as an opening in a crowded goal.

Whether using the instep kick for height or for accuracy, the approach to the ball is pretty much the same. The run-up positions for both kick are practically identical. Approach the ball slightly from the side, making sure that your left foot is placed alongside the ball. The foot placement is important. If your foot is too far behind the ball you will overbalance and the ball will only be scooped weakly into the air. If your foot is placed in front of the ball you will end up kicking the ball into the ground. Place your foot correctly so that you can swing your right leg through and contact the ball cleanly with the top of your foot.

Although the standing foot is very important when kicking a soccer ball, most people ignore it and concentrate only on the kicking foot. But at one point in the kick, the body weight and therefore the balance is entirely on the standing foot. You need superior balance to play soccer, and a quick way to develop it is to pay attention to the way you place your standing foot. It also helps to have both the knees bent just before and upon contact with the ball.

For accurate kicking both knees should be bent as the kicking foot is sweeping in to meet the ball. At the moment of contact, the knee of the kicking foot should be over the ball. After contact and upon follow-through the kicking leg will straighten.

For the lofted kick, the knees are again bent. However, the knee of the kicking foot is behind the ball more on this kick than for accuracy kicking as the kicking foot must get partially underneath the ball to make it rise. Beginning players tend to kick stiff-legged, which makes for poor balance and accuracy. Watch the way professionals bend their knees when they kick. They stay well balanced and they kick through the ball smoothly and efficiently. It has a lot to do with the bent knees.

There are several details to be learned here, but you can avoid confusion if you get your priorities straight.

● First, get the approach to the ball and the placement of the standing foot right. Approach slightly from the side and place the standing foot beside or slightly behind the ball. The kicking foot should swing through the ball smoothly and efficiently.

● Second, you must get contact with the ball with your whole instep—the top of the foot, not the toe. Don't worry if you can't make the ball go the direction you want. As long as you are kicking the ball with your instep, accuracy will come with practice and perseverance.

LOFTED PASS

Run-up, slightly from side.
The left foot is well positioned
on the side and slightly behind
the ball.
Eyes are on the ball.
Arms are thrust out for bal-
ance.
Knees are bent.
Kicking ankle is flexed, al-
though not so much as for
accuracy kicking.

Instep is fitted snugly under-
neath and partially around the
ball. Ankle is flexed.
Knee of kicking foot is slightly
behind the ball.
Heel lower on contact than for
accuracy kicking.
On contact, eyes are on ball,
body weight is transferred to
kicking foot.

Lift.
Ball has begun to lift.
Body inclining backwards
to help lift.

Follow-through.

ACCURACY KICKING

*Run-up, slightly from the side.
Left foot is at side of ball.
Head over ball. Eyes on ball.
The instep is perfectly placed
to kick through the center of
the casing.
On contact ball, knee and head
will form a perfect line.
Arms are spread for balance.
The kicker is over the ball so
as to keep the ball low.*

*Side view on contact.
Ankle flexed, toe down and
heel up.
Knee over ball.
Ball will travel low and straight.
On contact eyes should be on
ball.
Ball, knee and head form per-
fect line.*

Left foot is alongside ball, toe of standing foot pointing towards target.
Right foot is swinging through to meet the ball.
Knee is over ball.
Ball will travel low and straight towards reader.

Instep fitted neatly into the center casing of the ball.
Standing foot pointing towards target.
Ball will keep low.
Balance is on standing foot.

EXERCISE 1 (LEVEL 1)

Requirements: Boys of approximately equal kicking strengths, in pairs. Distance between pairs is five to 20 yards, depending upon kicking strengths. One ball per pair. (Line method)

For this exercise, simply have your boys kick a stationary ball between one another using their insteps. The ball should be stationary so that they can work on their timing and foot placement, etc. Your job is to see that your boys approach the ball slightly from the side, and that they use their insteps. The boy receiving the ball controls it and plays it back to his partner in the same manner.

Inevitably some boys will continue to kick with their toes. You have to convince them that the instep kick is superior to the toe kick. These boys will regress before they note improvement through instep kicking, for they have to adjust to a new method. This will complicate your task, but stick to it anyway. The end product will be well worth the time and effort.

As your boys improve at kicking a stationary ball, advance to Exercise two.

EXERCISE 2 (LEVEL 2)

Requirements: The same as in Exercise 1.

The boy with the ball pushes it slightly to his side and in front of himself, and advances to kick the now moving ball to his partner. The boy receiving the ball controls it and plays the ball back to his partner in the same manner. Continue the practice making sure that your boys maintain their distance apart.

As your boys improve at this skill, define and practice the differences in the two methods of instep kicking. For a period coach accuracy kicking, stressing the importance of keeping the ball low. Having impressed your point, move on to a lofted passing exercise. Stress the importance of gaining height by placing the instep of the kicking foot partially underneath the ball while leaning the body back slightly on contact.

It may be necessary to go back to kicking stationary balls for these practices. If this is the case, progress to kicking a moving ball as your boys show improvement.

At a time you think opportune, instruct your boys to use their other, weaker foot.

I have only given two instep kicking exercises, which I suggest your team practice for 10 minutes every training session. This is because I recommend, at the end of each training session, a 10- to 20-minute game. In these games, your boys will have to play with and adjust to a moving ball. Encourage them to kick it the first time whenever possible. In this manner they will get a great deal of kicking practice.

Initially these games will be kicking matches, so stress kicking the ball correctly and meeting the ball. As the season progresses, your boys will improve and you will find that you can advance to other skills, i.e., heading, controlling the ball, etc., while still being able to practice kicking.

Instep kicking can be practiced during shooting practice.

The kicking foot is flexed for the lofted pass kick. However, it is not flexed as much as for the accuracy kick. Compare photos of both kicks at the moment of contact.

The lofted pass can be as accurate as the accuracy kick. The difference, apart from height, is travelling time.

Young players sometimes have problems getting the knee of their kicking foot over the ball on accuracy kicking. If they do have this problem, tell them to get their head over the ball. Then if they keep their toe down and heel up their knee will automatically be over the ball on contact.

The last stride with the standing foot, before placing it beside or slightly behind the ball, is most important. It will decide whether the kick will be smooth or ragged. I call the last stride the compensation stride for if you are near the ball, your stride must be short; if you are not near, your stride will be long, therefore your last stride compensates for your position in relation to the ball. It is usually a long stride.

The reason many students kick with their toes is that their standing foot is way behind the ball. It is then very difficult for them to kick with their instep. Make sure that the standing foot is in the correct position. I know we have already mentioned this point, but as it is so important, I know you won't mind my stressing it again.

The Inside of the Foot Pass

The inside of the foot pass can be used, by proficient players, for fairly long distance passing and even for shooting. It is mainly used, however, for short, accurate, along the ground passing, which is what we are interested in for now.

The more of the foot you can place on the ball at the moment of contact the more control you will have over where it goes.

The kicking area is the fleshy part of the inside of the foot between the big toe and the heel bone. That's a lot of foot with which to guide the ball accurately to where you want it to go.

When using this kick, strike the ball in the center of the casing. This will keep it low and straight. Leaning back on contact and placing the kicking foot under the ball will cause it to rise. When using this kick, remember that the ball will go where the inside of your foot is facing at the moment of contact. So if you want the ball to arrive at its intended destination have your kicking foot level with the target. This kick is very similar to a golf putt in control and accuracy. You use the inside of your foot in exactly the same way as you would use a putter.

Look up to see where to pass.
Head over the ball.
Right foot poised to strike through ball.
Left foot alongside ball, toe turned inward.
Knees bent, the right far more than the left.
On contact, having the body over the ball will keep the ball low.

Inside of the foot to ball contact.
Ball is being played in the center of it's casing.
On contact, eyes should be on the ball.
Ball will stay low.

Follow-through shown from side.

Slightly exaggerated follow-through shown from the front.

EXERCISE 3 (LEVEL 1)

Requirements: Boys in pairs, three yards apart. One ball per pair. (Line Method)

This exercise is a simple one. Have your boys pass a stationary ball between one another.

In their pairs, your boys pass the ball back and forth using the inside of the foot pass. The boy receiving the ball controls it and passes it back to his partner. Continue the exercise in this manner, advancing to greater distance between your boys and more pace on the ball as they improve. The pass should be firm and accurate, not so weak that it just reaches the target, and not a cannonball that knocks the receiver over. Practice this skill with both feet.

If one ball per pair is not possible, form your boys in threes and fours and use the same exercise. One passes to two, two passes to three, and so on.

EXERCISE 4 (LEVEL 1)

Requirements: The same as in Exercise 3.

In their pairs, your boys alternately attempt to sidefoot the ball through their partners' legs. The boy receiving the ball stands with his legs wide apart. His partner sidefoots the ball towards him. The receiver stops the ball with his feet as it is going wide or with his hands if it is going through his legs, and he, in turn, attempts to sidefoot the ball through his partner's legs, which should now be apart. Continue the practice in this manner, advancing to greater distance between your boys as they improve. Practice this skill with both feet.

To make this exercise into a game, ask for the first boy to score five through the leg goals. Raise the number at a later date.

EXERCISE 5 (LEVEL 2)

Requirements: The same as in exercise 3 and 4.

(Advance to this exercise only when your boys have shown improvement at exercises 3 and 4.)

In their pairs, your boys attempt to pass the ball back and forth without first pausing to control the ball. See how many consecutive first time passes they can make before the sequence breaks down.

This is more demanding than the previous two exercises at your boys must now adjust to a moving ball. Practice this skill with both feet.

Increase the distance between your boys as they improve.

EXERCISE 6 (LEVEL 3)

Requirements: One stake. One ball.

Hammer the stake into the ground. Form your boys into a circle around the stake, each at a distance of three yards. The idea is to try to knock the stake out of the ground. A boy gets one point for hitting the stake and two for completely knocking it out of the ground.

To begin with, instruct your boys to control and then play the ball. After this has been satisfactorily done, advance to first time passing. An additional advancement is to have your boys jog around the outside of the circle as the ball is being played. They have to adjust quickly to the ball and play it the first time. Stress to them that they must play the ball with whatever foot the ball comes to. On the command, "Change," the group turns and runs the opposite way around the circle. When they have progressed, increase the distance from the stake and advance to using two balls.

EXERCISE 7 (LEVEL 3)

Requirements: Boys in pairs, three to five yards apart. One ball per pair.

In this exercise your boys, in pairs, have to advance the length of the soccer field, or a similar area, by passing the ball to each other.

The boy with the ball passes it to his partner and advances. The boy receiving the ball controls it and passes it to his partner in his now-advanced position. Having played the ball, the boy who received it must advance to await a pass from his partner. In this fashion they advance down the field. At first this practice will be jumpy and jerky, for your boys have to time their runs as well as adjust to a moving ball. Aim for smooth continuous practices whereby as soon as a boy passes the ball he runs forward to receive it from his partner. Practice this skill with both feet. (See diagram.)

EXERCISE 7

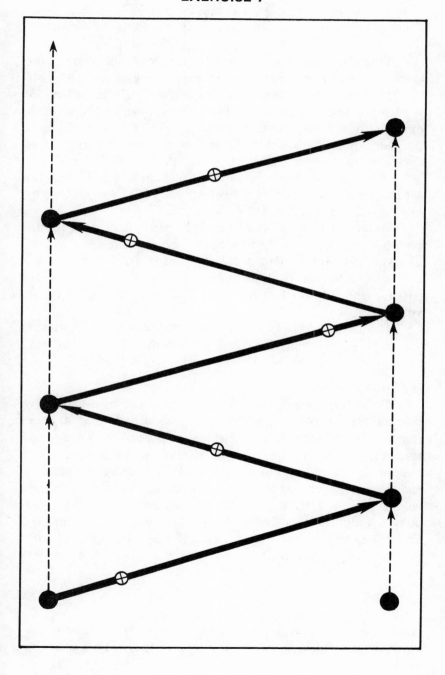

Heading

You head a soccer ball with your forehead, which is not only the most convenient part of your head (being in line with your eyes), but also the hardest. Don't use the top, side, or back of your head, for, apart from the fact that you can't see the ball to direct it, the resulting contact can be painful. Keep your eyes on the ball, for it is moving in the air and is liable to change direction, even in the shortest space.

Many soccer players are afraid of heading at first. This is a natural tendency which is transitory and will be overcome by playing and practicing.

Watch out! Here comes the ball. As it is coming toward you, look around quickly to see what options are open to you. Can you play the ball to a colleague or could you head for a goal? Quickly look back at the ball and adjust to it. Whenever possible, move to the ball and meet it. Don't wait for it to meet you.

Having moved to the ball, tense your neck muscles, making sure that your tongue is behind your clenched teeth, and play the ball with your forehead. On contact you will blink.

Defensive Heading

Defenders, or players in a defensive position, usually have one main requirement when heading a soccer ball; that is, to get the ball as far away from their goal as possible. In congested areas this means they have to get as much height on the ball as possible, for they cannot take the risk of heading the ball low and having it intercepted by the opposing team. To obtain height, a player must get partially underneath the ball (not completely underneath so that he heads the ball straight up into the air for it to return to the same spot). Having gotten partially under the ball, he must also try to power it away from the danger area.

Many soccer players are afraid of heading at first. This is a natural tendency which is transitory and will be overcome by playing and practicing.

The power to do this comes from the neck muscles. The player, knowing he is going to play the ball, tenses his neck muscles and pulls his head slightly back. When the ball is within playing distance, he jerks his head forward to meet it and guide it to its destination. The distance the ball will travel depends upon its original speed and the power of the header.

Attacking Heading (Heading for Goal)

Players heading for goal worry defenders, and goalkeepers in particular, by heading the ball down and into the corners of goals. In a congested penalty area, a ball in the air is seen far easier than a ball hidden amidst a tangle of legs. Goalkeepers prefer to see the ball headed high up into the air, for with their hand and reach advantage matters become easier for them. On the ground it's an entirely different matter. They have to stretch their backs to get a low shot and, once on the floor, it's difficult for them to get up quickly. There is also the added advantage to forwards of the rebound. A ball can rebound off a post or a leg. Forwards should head low and also to the corners of the goal.

Jumping to Head

Jumping to head a soccer ball requires more coordination than heading with both feet firmly planted on the ground. The difference is timing. A player must time his jump so that he meets the ball as it arrives near him. There is less time to adjust to the ball. If you jump too early or too late you will in all probability miss the ball, as you have to land before you can readjust and it will have passed by on its way by then. The player must learn to assess the speed of the ball and to jump so that he meets it at the correct moment.

Adjusting to ball.
Eyes on ball.
Forehead poised to meet the ball.

Head going forward to meet ball.
Forehead is in correct position.
Eyes on ball.
Neck muscles tensed.

Forehead to ball contact.
Teeth clenched.
Tongue inside teeth.

EXERCISE 8 (LEVEL 1)

Requirements: Boys in pairs, three yards apart. One ball per pair. (Line Method)

This exercise will help give your boys the confidence to head a soccer ball. The boy with the ball gently lobs or throws it to his partner's head. His partner heads the ball back to him. After 10 heads the boys change functions so that the server now heads the ball 10 times. Increase the distance between your boys as they improve.

EXERCISE 9 (LEVEL 2)

Requirements: One ball per boy.

This exercise will also help build confidence. Instruct your boys to head their ball as many times as they can before it hits the ground. A player starts this practice by lobbing or throwing the ball onto his head.

To increase interest, ask for the boy with the largest number of consecutive heads. You will find the most successful in this skill will be the boys who keep the ball close to their foreheads. This could be used as a regular loosening-up drill to get a feel of the ball. A ball between two, three or more boys with each boy having a turn at this exercise could easily be worked if you don't have enough balls for a ball per boy.

EXERCISE 10 (LEVEL 3)

Requirements: The same as in Exercise 9.

See how many consecutive headers each pair can obtain before the ball hits the ground. One boy starts the practice by lobbing or throwing the ball to his partner. The boys head the ball back and forth as many times as they can. This is an advance from exercise 9 as your boys now have to adjust constantly to a moving ball from a partner.

Dribbling

The art of dribbling (and it is an art) is a major part of a soccer player's make-up. It is such an important skill that it should be practiced as much as possible.

It is exciting to be able to dribble well, and if this skill is allied to the team effort it can be a very telling factor.

The purpose of dribbling is to hold the ball when it cannot be passed advantageously and to maneuver (dribble) it until it can be used effectively against the opposing team, i.e., by passing it when a favorable position is reached, or getting into a position for a shot at the goal.

Arangiz of Miami is running with the ball because he cannot pass it to advantage. Sharp (No. 10) is sprinting toward the goal for a pass. (John Pineda photo).

Peripheral vision, the ability to see all around you, also plays a big part in dribbling. It enables you to watch the field of play, and see the ball at the same time. Many youngsters get the ball caught directly underneath their bodies. Since they then need their full attention to watch the ball, they lose track of the nearby opponents and the developing play around them. If the ball is in front of them they can see both the ball and the developing play. This is very important.

You should dribble until a favorable situation develops which you have the chance to exploit. The other team won't stand still and let you dribble past them; they will challenge you for the ball. This means you will have to beat them and this is in itself a high skill. To fake an opponent out is difficult, to fake an opponent out and still retain possession of the ball is even harder. This is where balance comes in (see photo on next page) and where dribbling becomes a very high skill.

Close and Long Dribbling

Dribbling is divided into two categories, close and long.

Close dribbling is designed for controlling the ball in small congested areas. To begin with, use the insides of both feet for close dribbling. Having reached a reasonable proficiency, add the outsides of both feet combining your control of the ball with an occasional body swerve will give you a formidable weapon to add to your armory of skills.

Long dribbling is used mainly for speed. For instance, if a flank man sees a gap in the defense, he pushes the ball into the gap, usually with the outside of his foot, and then he sprints after it. It should be a controlled pass and not a blind kick so that he can reach the ball before it has gone out of play.

A ball that is played travels faster than a ball that is dribbled. Therefore, only dribble when you cannot pass the ball to your team's advantage.

Davy Carlton beat his man during the 1972 season's Dallas vs. Miami NASL game at Texas Stadium. Davy's body swerve and balance are perfect as he steers the ball away from the groping foot of his opponent. Davy has beaten his man by having the ball under his close control and baiting his opponent to lunge in. This is exactly what Davy wanted. He was ready to move away from the tackle by pushing the ball away from the danger area with the outside of his right foot.

Davy has played the ball in a controlled fashion. Notice how close he is to the ball. He has not kicked it too far in front of him. This is an example of good close control.

His next move is to look up and reassess the situation.

*Inside of
foot dribbling*

*Outside of
foot dribbling*

EXERCISE 11 (LEVEL 1)

Requirements: One stake. One ball.

Hammer the stake into the ground. Form your boys into a line, one behind the other, facing the stake at a distance of 15 to 20 yards. The first boy dribbles the ball up to the stake, around it, and back to the front of the line where he stops it dead for the next boy to go.

Each boy in the line repeats the process. Repeat two or more times.

This exercise can be made competitive by dividing your group into two teams, and having a race (if there is an odd number, one boy on one team can go twice). Simply add another ball and stake, or have both teams use the same stake. Stress to your boys that they should use both feet when dribbling.

EXERCISE 12 (LEVEL 2)

Requirements: Six stakes. One ball.

Place six stakes, three long strides apart, in a straight line. Line up your boys behind the first stake. Singly, starting at the first stake, each boy dribbles in and out of the stakes until he reaches the last one, which he dribbles around. He then dribbles the ball straight back to the first stake, as fast as he can go, making sure he has control of the ball as he must stop it dead for the next boy to go. He does not dribble in and out of the stakes on the way back. As your boys improve, place the stakes irregularly.

Timing this exercise is a good way of measuring improvement and stimulating interest. It is essential that your boys keep the ball close to them while dribbling in and out of the stakes. Remind them to use both feet.

EXERCISE 13 (LEVEL 2)

Requirements: One ball per boy.

Have your boys stand an equal distance apart in a circle.

The center-circle of a soccer field would be ideal for this practice.

Instruct them to dribble at a slow pace around the circle. As they continue dribbling, explain to them that they are going to work on the whistle. On one whistle, your boys must stop their ball dead, turn around, and dribble back the way they came. If your boys were dribbling clockwise, on one whistle they should stop and dribble counter-clockwise.

Work your boys on one whistle for two minutes, stressing the coaching points of keeping the ball close in front of them and using both feet.

On two whistles, your boys must stop their ball dead, leave it, run forward to the next ball, which has been left by the boy in front of them, and carry on dribbling. Work on two whistles for two minutes.

Now combine work on one and two whistles for one minute.

On three whistles, your boys must stop their ball dead, leave it, turn and run back to the ball behind them and then turn again and carry on dribbling in the same direction.

Work on three whistles for two minutes.

Now combine work on one, two, and three whistles for two minutes.

As your boys improve, gradually increase the tempo. As the tempo increases it will be harder to maintain an even distance between them. Keep hammering home that they must use both feet to dribble with.

Don't work your boys too hard when they first try this exercise. Break them in slowly. After a few sessions their ball control and their reactions will improve noticeably.

If you don't have enough balls for a ball per boy, divide your group in half. Organize a 4- or 5-a-side game with one half of your boys while the other half practice Exercise 13. At the completion of working on the whistle, the groups can change functions.

EXERCISE 14 (LEVEL 3)

Requirements: The same as in Exercise 13.

A penalty area would be ideal for this series of exercises. If you only have a spare piece of ground, mark out an area with traffic cones or stakes or whatever, of an approximately equal size (about 18 x 44 yards).

EXERCISE 14 (Part One)

Instruct your boys to dribble their ball anywhere in the penalty area. Tell them that on hearing the whistle they must stop their ball dead by placing the sole of their foot on it. On the first whistle a few boys will take longer to control their balls. This is the time to stress the point of keeping the ball under close control.

Work on five to 10 whistles.

EXERCISE 14 (Part Two)

On the whistle your boys must stop their ball, turn, and go back the way they came.

Work on five to 10 whistles.

EXERCISE 14 (Part Three)

On the whistle your boys must fake out an imaginary opponent. Tell them to make it as real as possible. Soccer players need imagination.

Work on five to 10 whistles.

EXERCISE 14 (Part Four)

On the whistle offer yourself as an opponent to your boys. Tell them to try to fake you out. Offer passive resistance, but kick away any balls that come too close to you. If you have an assistant, have him offer passive resistance also.

EXERCISE 14 (Part Five)

On the whistle your boys must dribble in and out of each other, as close as they possibly can without colliding. Tell them to stop when you whistle, and to spread out to wait for the next whistle. On the whistle they again dribble in and out of each other.

Work on five to 10 whistles.

Having completed the five parts of Exercise 14, reduce your area to the confines of the goalkeeper's area or the six-yard box. Now repeat the five parts of Exercise 14.

Your boys' space is now very much restricted so it is essential for them to exercise close control.

EXERCISE 14 (Part Six)

So far the dribbling exercises have been without real opposition. In part six opposition is added.

Tell your boys to dribble anywhere in the goalkeeper's area. (If you have a large group—I know that some coaches coach two teams—use the penalty area for this game.) On the whistle any boy can kick any other boy's ball out of the goal area. Once a boy's ball is kicked out of the goal area he ceases to take part in the game and cannot kick any other boy's ball. Once out of the game a player leaves the goal area. The last boy left with his ball is the winner.

This game demands that a boy keep his ball under close control while constantly looking around to see if he is being threatened, and if he can get a chance to kick another boy's ball away. A boy's tackling can improve by playing this game.

It might take your boys a few attempts to get used to it.

Repeat three times or more.

Exercise 14 can last from 30 minutes upwards and could last an entire practice session. This is up to the coach. Keep on reminding your boys to use both of their feet.

The Sole of the Foot Control

The sole of the foot control is used for controlling balls moving along the ground or dropping out of the air. You control the ball by wedging it between the sole of your controlling foot and the ground. When you place your foot on the ball be careful not to stab at it; if you do so, you will overbalance and probably fall over. Place the sole of your controlling foot, firmly and evenly, on the top of the ball so that you cover it with approximately the front half of your foot. Ideally the ball should be stopped in front of your body. If you stop it underneath your body, you have to drag it out and lose vital seconds. If you stop it too far in front of you, you tend to overbalance.

Your foot must control the dropping ball at the precise moment it touches the ground. Your margin of error is small. Position your foot near the area where the ball is going to drop. As the ball hits the ground, place the sole of your controlling foot on it. This will stop the ball from bouncing away and keep it under your control. If the ball is coming to you along the ground, simply wedge it. Don't hold your controlling foot so high that the ball runs underneath it.

Right foot prepares to control dropping ball.
Sole of controlling foot is raised to spred over the ball.
Left foot and arms are balancing body.
Ball will be controlled in front of body.
Eyes are on the ball.

Ball which has dropped under control in front of body.
On contact, eyes should be on the ball.

*Sole of foot controlling ball
played along ground.
Front 1/3 of foot in contact
with ball.
Eyes on ball.*

EXERCISE 15 (LEVEL 1)

Requirements: Boys in pairs, 3 yards apart. One ball per pair. (Line Method)

In their pairs your boys pass the ball firmly to one another along the ground. The receiver attempts to control the ball with the sole of his foot and then passes the ball back to his partner who attempts the same. Continue the practice in this manner, increasing the distance apart and the pace of the service as your boys improve. Practice this control with both feet.

One half of this exercise consists of passing, so although you are coaching sole of the foot control don't forget to look for passing points as well.

EXERCISE 16 (LEVEL 2)

Requirements: The same as in Exercise 15.

In their pairs your boys gently lob or throw the ball back and forth. The boy receiving the ball adjusts to the ball and attempts to control it with the sole of his foot as it touches the ground. He then gently lobs or throws the ball back to his partner who attempts to control it in the same fashion. Continue the practice in this manner advancing to higher throws and greater distance between your boys as they improve. Practice this control with both feet.

The Inside of the Foot Control

Because the inside of the foot is large and fleshy, it is the area most used by players to control a soccer-ball. It is exactly the same area as used for passing with the inside of the foot. You control the ball by meeting it with the inside of the foot. At the moment of contact slightly relax and withdraw your controlling foot. (Don't relax too much so that your foot hangs loose). This cushioning effect takes the pace out of the ball and enables you, with practice, to control it as soon as it touches your foot. Relaxing your foot slightly on contact is very important; a ball will bounce away from a rigid surface.

This skill is mainly used to control balls played along the ground. However, it can also be used to control balls which are dropping. The principle is the same, the only difference being that your controlling foot and knee will be higher so as to meet the ball (see photo page 40). A slight backward lean helps you here as it enables you to present a wider control area to the ball.

Meeting the ball in the middle of the casing.
Eyes on ball.
Left foot balancing body.
Knees slightly bent.

Ball is under control.
Controlling foot has withdrawn, taking the pace out of the ball.
Eyes on the ball.

Controlling foot raised to meet the ball in the air.
Eyes on ball.
The inside of the controlling foot is in line with the fall of the ball and is turned out to present a wide surface for control.
Slight backward body lean.

EXERCISE 17 (LEVEL 1)

Requirements: Boys in pairs, three yards apart. One ball per pair. (Line Method)

In their pairs your boys pass the ball firmly to one another along the ground. The boy receiving the ball attempts to control it with the inside of his foot and pass it back to his partner who will attempt the same. Continue the practice in this manner, increasing the distance between your boys and the pace of the service as they improve. Practice this control with both feet.

EXERCISE 18 (LEVEL 2)

Requirements: The same as in Exercise 17.

In their pairs your boys gently lob or throw the ball back and forth at around waist height. The boy receiving the ball adjusts to it and attempts to control it with the inside of his foot. He then gently lobs or throws the ball back to his partner who attempts to control it in the same fashion. Continue the practice in this manner, advancing to a greater distance between your boys as they improve. Practice this control with both feet.

The Instep Control

This method of control is used, almost exclusively, to control balls which are dropping from the sky. Once again, meet the ball firmly, by lifting and extending your controlling foot, which relaxes slightly on contact. Now lower your controlling foot and you will find that with practice the ball will follow your foot down to the ground and you will have control of it.

If your controlling foot is stiff on contact, the ball will bounce well out of your immediate range of control.

Eyes on ball.
Knee of controlling foot beginning to rise to meet dropping ball.

Contact
Eyes on ball.
Left foot balancing body.

Eyes on ball.
On contact, controlling foot
relaxes and lowers ball.
Ball has dropped as if drawn
by magnet.

Look up.
Ball is now under control in
front of the body and well
within playing distance.

EXERCISE 19 (LEVEL 2)

Requirements: Boys in pairs, three yards apart. One ball per pair. (Line Method)

In their pairs your boys gently lob or throw the ball back and forth. The boy receiving the ball adjusts to it and attempts to control it with his instep. He then gently lobs or throws the ball back to his partner who attempts to control the ball in the same fashion. Continue the practice in this manner advancing to higher throws as your boys improve. Practice this control with both feet.

The Thigh Control

The thigh is a very fleshy part of the anatomy and as such is ideal for controlling a soccer ball.

You control the ball in the middle of the fleshy area of your thigh, avoiding the bony knee. Beginners always manage to get the knee in the way so that the ball flies in all directions. On contact, relax and withdraw your thigh and the ball will drop in front of your body. This is again the cushioning effect.

As a general rule, to control balls which are dropping keep the controlling thigh level with the ground by raising the knee to hip level (see photo below). On contact the ball will slightly rise before dropping to the ground.

Balls being played at the three- to four-foot level are controlled by only partially raising the knee of the controlling thigh (see following photo). By relaxing and withdrawing the thigh on contact, the ball will drop at your feet.

The ball will not drop at your feet and stay there for you. It will need to be controlled by another part of your anatomy (the instep, for instance) before being completely under your control.

Eyes on ball.
Thigh contact to dropping ball.
Left foot balancing body.
Arms spread, partially for balance and partially to avoid handling the ball should it bounce awkwardly.

Thigh contact to ball played
at the three to four foot level.
Eyes on ball.
Left foot balancing body.
Knee of controlling thigh
drawn halfway to hip level.

Ball dropping in front of body
after contact.
Eyes still on ball.

EXERCISE 20 (LEVEL 2)

Requirements: Boys in pairs, three yards apart. One ball per pair. (Line Method)

In their pairs, your boys gently lob or throw the ball back and forth, aiming for the general area of the thigh. The boy receiving the ball adjusts to it and attempts to control it with his thigh. He then gently lobs or throws the ball back to his partner who attempts to control the ball in the same fashion. Continue the practice in this manner advancing to higher throws as your boys improve. Practice this control with both thighs.

The Chest Control

Controlling a soccer ball with the chest is very similar to heading in that the players are wary of the skill until they have actually tried it. Don't be afraid. There is no reason to shy away from the ball. Place your body firmly in the path of the ball and, once again using the cushioning effect, relax your chest on contact. This will take the pace out of the ball and it will drop in front of your body.

As with the thigh control, once the ball has dropped to your feet it still needs an extra touch to control it completely.

This skill requires timing and practice and will take longer to master than most other skills. Boys will tend to let the ball go by them or head it rather than chest it. The skill will emerge gradually. Persevere as it is well worth the time and effort.

Meeting the ball at 3/4 chest height.
Eyes on the ball.
Chest to ball contact.
Arms spread to avoid handling ball should it bounce awkwardly.
Feet spread for balance.
Slight forward lean of body will direct ball downwards.

Meeting the ball at full chest height.
Eyes on ball.
Arms spread to avoid handling ball.

*Meeting ball at just above chest
height.
Eyes on ball.
Adjusting to awkward height of
of ball by standing on toes.
Arms spread for balance and to
avoid handling should the ball
bounce awkwardly.
Body balanced by toes and
arms.*

EXERCISE 21 (LEVEL 2)

*Requirements: Boys in pairs, three yards apart. One ball
per pair. (Line Method)*

In their pairs your boys gently lob or throw the ball back
and forth, aiming for the general area of the chest. The boy receiving the ball adjusts to it and attempts to control it with his
chest. He then gently lobs or throws the ball back to his partner
who attempts to control the ball in the same fashion. Continue
the practice in this manner, advancing to a greater distance between your boys as they improve.

Many associations allow girls to substitute a crossed-arms
action for the chesting action. Both arms must be held tightly
across the chest, with opposite fists on opposite shoulders. The
arms cannot be held out from the chest and cannot thrust at the
ball. Check with your local association on this point.

*Kyle Rote, Jr. chesting the ball at a difficult height. 1974 NASL season,
Los Angeles Aztecs vs. Dallas Tornado. (M. Julius Baum photo)*

Tackling

You have learned how to kick, how to pass, head, and how to control a soccer ball! GOOD! But the other team has the ball and you can use none of these skills until you gain possession. How do you gain possession? By one of three methods: your opponents pass it badly and thus give it to you; you intelligently intercept; or you win the ball by tackling for it.

Tackling requires timing, determination and strength.

Timing a tackle is a skill which will improve with experience and practice. Once your timing has improved, then you can use your determination and strength. Forwards love defenders who lunge in at them when they have full control of the ball. They dislike a defender who gets close to the ball, not too close as to get caught flat and be beaten, but close enough to put pressure on them. Then, a slight miscalculation or miscontrol of the ball enables the defender to tackle at the most advantageous time to him. Now is the time for determination and strength. The defender has chosen the time to tackle and whether it is a block tackle or a quick kick with the toe it gives the tackling team a chance to win the ball or to make the opposition lose possession of it. When making foot to ball contact the ankle of the tackling foot should be locked, not loose. The tackler's eyes should be on the ball.

Block Tackle

You block tackle by placing the inside of your tackling foot against the ball (see diagram A) while your opponent tries to play it or block it himself. If two players meet the ball evenly the more determined tackler will usually win the tackle. However, you will very seldom see a 50-50 block tackle. Most block tackles are favorable to one side, but, remember, many tackles are won by players refusing to be defeated by odds. And don't worry about being hurt if you go in strongly for a ball. The people who get hurt are those who go in half-heartedly.

You block tackle the ball in the middle of the casing making sure that your body and head are over the ball on contact, your tackling ankle is locked, and your eyes are on the ball.

Diagram A

You then play through the ball with your body weight. Often a ball becomes stuck between two determined players. This is where the follow-up technique is required. Still maintaining contact, quickly lower your tackling foot underneath the ball and try to roll or flick it over your opponent's foot. This sudden change from force to subtleness can prove to be very effective by overbalancing an opponent and giving you a moment's lapse on which to capitalize.

Slide Tackle

The slide tackle is designed to dispossess an opponent when a block tackle is not possible. It must be executed correctly, for once you're committed you will find yourself on the ground. If you miss your tackle you will then be out of the immediate action.

It is most important to time your tackle properly. Make sure you tackle across the front of your opponent with the foot furthest from him ready to play the ball away. (This allows for the traveling distance of the ball from the start to finish of your tackle.) On slide tackling, the contact area of your foot to the ball will almost certainly be your instep.

Beware of slide tackling in your penalty area, as a miscalculation by you could lead to a penalty kick being awarded against your team. So be careful.

When the Ball is in Contention

Most soccer players can play fairly well when they are allowed the time and space to control the ball. It takes a good player to perform well when he has an opponent contesting him for every ball before he has it under control. Therefore try to deny an opponent time and space. Whenever possible crowd him, make life difficult for him. Remember—it's far easier to destroy than create.

EXERCISE 22—BLOCK TACKLING (LEVEL 1)

Requirements: Boys in pairs, two yards apart. One ball per pair (line method).

This exercise is designed to introduce your boys gently to the block tackle.

The ball should be placed between your boys in their pairs. The boys should each be two steps from the ball. Explain to them that they must time their approach so that they both make gentle contact with the ball at the same time, so that it becomes blocked between them. Give them time to adjust their timing and placement of feet. Having achieved these points (and it may well take a few sessions), move on to harder and harder contact with the ball. Over a period of weeks gradually introduce the technique of block tackling. It is good for your boys to practice both right and left foot blocking.

This simple exercise can be practiced in groups of three and four if not enough balls are available for a ball per pair.

When practicing block tackling make right foot to right foot contact or left to left foot contact.

EXERCISE 23—SLIDE TACKLING (LEVEL 2)

Requirements: Boys of approximately equal speed, in pairs. One ball per pair.

The boy with the ball runs in a straight line. His partner runs alongside him and slide tackles the ball away. The boys return to the start and change functions. Let each pair go individually as this gives you a chance to see every boy tackling.

This is an introductory exercise designed to show your boys what a slide tackle is. To begin with, let the boy running with the ball offer only passive resistance. This allows the boy who is slide tackling to time his tackle. As your boys get the feel of the tackle give the boy running with the ball a set distance to cover, e.g. 20 yards. Once he has covered the set distance he cannot be tackled. This gives the practice a touch of competition and helps to create a match situation.

On hard grounds slide tackling is limited in use, the block tackle being used more often. The slide tackle tends to be used more on wet grounds as moisture helps to reduce the friction as one's body hits the ground at the end of the tackle. This helps to stop any bad grazing which can occur by slide tackling on bone-hard grounds.

EXERCISE 24 (LEVEL 3)

Requirements: Group divided into two facing, sitting lines. Distance between lines 10 yards. Distance between boys on same line two yards. One ball per group.

Starting from opposite ends, number both teams from 1 upward, i.e. with 16 boys, the boys numbered 1 would sit facing the boys numbered 8 of the opposite team. Place the ball between the two lines, in the center, an equal distance from both teams.

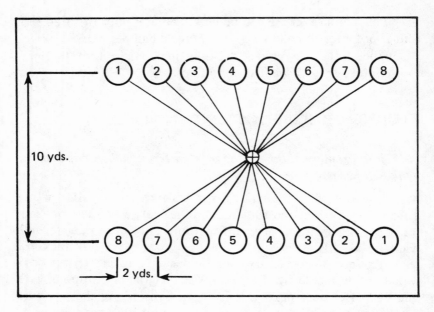

To start the game, call a number. Both boys having that number must try to gain possession of the ball and dribble it back to their own line. If a boy crosses his line with the ball under control he gains his team a point. His opponent of course will try to stop him and dribble the ball over his line. This produces some hearty tackling which is really the object of the game. End any pair's practice if they kick the ball out of the area where your boys are sitting. Replace the ball and call another number.

This exercise offers opportunities for both block and slide tackling.

After a few sessions, by which time your boys will have become used to the exercise, call out two numoers at a time. By having 2 vs. 2, you have a game situation which becomes more than just a tackling exercise although still offering many opportunities for tackling.

As already mentioned, dribbling Exercise 14 (Part 6) can also be used for tackling practice.

You don't always have to tackle your opponent to get the ball. Sometimes you can get it just by closing the distance. By staying close to your opponent, you can take advantage of his getting flustered and losing control of the ball.

Even professional soccer players do this. Staying close to

the man with the ball puts all the pressure on him. It can often force him into taking chances. At the very least, it puts the defender in the position to take immediate advantage of lapses. For instance, the man with the ball may kick it too far ahead of him, giving the defender the chance to intercept or tackle. This way the defender is tackling at the moment most advantageous to him.

Goalkeeping

The goalkeeper is the one truly specialized player on a soccer team. He is the only player allowed to handle the ball. This he can only do within the confines of his penalty area. The prerequisite for a goalkeeper is a safe pair of hands. He must also be brave, to dive at opponents' feet; agile, to enable him to throw himself at shots on his goal; and patiently attentive, as he

Kenny Cooper of the Dallas Tornado places his body behind the ball. His hands are cupped to hold the ball to his chest.

can be out of a game for a long period and then be called upon
to make a save. His reflexes must also be sharp for him to react
quickly to shots from close-in.

Once in possession of a soccer ball, the goalkeeper is allowed four steps before he must release it. This he can do by kicking, throwing or rolling the ball. Kicking is for distance, throwing or rolling are for accuracy and more limited advances. Some
goalkeepers, however, can throw the ball a great distance.

On many occasions a goalkeeper cannot hold a ball and
must punch it away or tip it over his goal. He should only try
to hold the ball when he has complete confidence that he can
do so. In a crowded penalty area, he is liable to catch the ball,
bump into players and drop it. He is many times better advised
to attempt to fist or punch the ball away. Two handed punching is safer than one handed punching as it gives a greater surface to connect with the ball, and thus greater accuracy.

Generally a goalkeeper should go for any ball inside his
goal-area or six-yard box.

● Goalkeepers are advised to always try to place their
bodies behind their hands when attempting a save. If the ball
should slip through their hands it could be blocked by their
bodies.

● Goalkeepers should stand at the goalpost farthest from
the ball when a corner-kick has been awarded against their team.
It is much easier for a goalkeeper to run forward and attempt to
meet a ball than to run back and attempt to play a ball going
over his head.

● It is wise to choose at least two goalkeepers for your
team. One boy may be a back-up and only used in emergencies
or both may have an equal amount of time in games.

● It can be difficult to coach your goalkeepers while trying
to keep the interest of your entire group. The alternatives are
to coach them at the conclusion of the practice or to have an
assistant coach them.

Narrowing the Angle:

In diagram "A" following, the goalkeeper has made the attacker's task fairly easy by staying on his goal line and showing
him the vast majority of the goal.

Diagram "B" following, shows the attacker in the same

position as in diagram "A." This time, however, the goalkeeper has advanced from his goal line and now the attacker has a smaller area to aim at. This is called narrowing the angle.

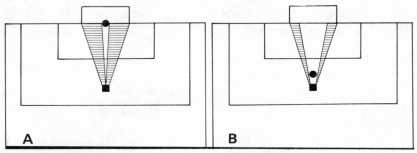

Large Target Area   *Small Target Area*

A goalkeeper who moves forward to meet an oncoming attacker forces the attacker to look at him, however momentarily, as well as at the ball. This helps to divide the attacker's attention and can cause him to miscontrol the ball or shoot hurriedly.

Goalkeepers should be careful not to run blindly at an attacker who has the ball under his control. It is a relatively simple task to sidestep him if he does. Having advanced and got near to the ball, a goalkeeper should spread himself and be prepared to go to either side. In a 1 vs. 1 situation goalkeepers should try always to have their eyes on the ball. (This, of course, applies to all situations but is particularly important with the ball so near to his goal and with no one to help him.)

The goalkeeping exercises are designed purely for goalkeepers. It would, however, be a good idea to take your entire group through the four parts of Exercise 25 so they can begin to appreciate what is required of a goalkeeper.

EXERCISE 25—Part One (LEVEL 1)

Requirements: Boys in pairs, three yards apart. One ball per pair. (Line Method)

In their pairs your boys roll the ball back and forth. The boy receiving the ball gathers it, as shown in Diagram C, and rolls it back to his partner. Continue the practice in this manner gradually increasing the pace of the service. Diagram F shows another method of taking a ground ball.

EXERCISE 25—Part Two

Repeat the same exercise as in part one with the exception that your boys now bounce throw the ball to one another. The boy receiving the ball collects it as shown in diagram D.

Increase the pace of the service gradually.

GROUND BALL

One knee bent. Palms facing the ball to draw it up to the protection of the body. If the ball slips through the hands it will hit either a foot or a thigh.

C

D

CHEST HIGH BALL

Catch with both hands and pull into chest.

GROUND BALL

Feet together. Body in line with the ball. Back bent. Arms stretched. Hands ready to lift ball into chest.

E

F

CATCHING AN OVERHEAD BALL

Keep eyes on ball. Spread fingers to stop ball slipping away.

EXERCISE 25—Part Three

Repeat the exercise as in parts one and two with the exception that your boys now lob or throw the ball just above their partners' heads. The boy receiving the ball must catch it and draw it into his chest, as shown in diagram E.

Increase the pace of the service gradually.

EXERCISE 25—Part Four

This part of Exercise 25 is a combination of parts one, two and three. Your boys continue to serve the ball to one another, making sure that their service is varied. The service can be rolled, bounced or thrown.

EXERCISE 26 (LEVEL 1)

Requirements: The same as in Exercise 25.

Repeat the four parts of Exercise 25 with the one difference that the boy receiving the ball stands with his back to the server. As soon as the server has released the ball he must shout "NOW." On the shout the receiver must turn and attempt to collect the ball.

This exercise is designed to increase reaction speed, so there is no need to increase the distance between your boys; only the pace of the service needs to be increased.

Your goalkeeper will have a great deal of practice when your outfield players have shooting practices.

Shooting

You have been shown all the necessary skills required for a novice soccer player, except shooting. A soccer team can be accomplished in many facets of the game but unless they consistently score goals they will not succeed. In the final analysis, goals decide games and the majority of goals are scored by shooting. I have, therefore, laid out five shooting practices. They can be lengthy but they are always enjoyable.

The instep kick is the kick used for shooting in the majority of cases. For shooting exercises detailed in this book, use the instep kick.

I have enjoyed coaching this particular skill more than any other. Once your boys have progressed at instep kicking, advance to the following practices.

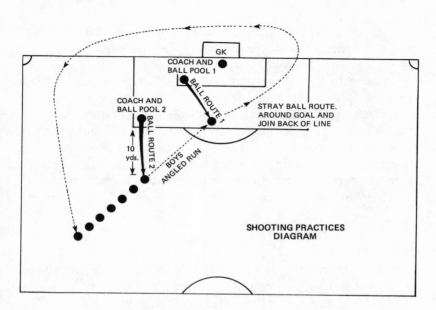

GK

COACH AND
BALL POOL 1

BALL ROUTE 1

COACH AND
BALL POOL 2

BALL ROUTE 2

STRAY BALL ROUTE.
AROUND GOAL AND
JOIN BACK OF LINE

10
yds.

BOYS
ANGLED RUN

SHOOTING PRACTICES
DIAGRAM

EXERCISE 27 (LEVEL 1)

Requirements: Boys in line, one behind the other. Front boy 10 yards outside of the penalty area (see diagram above). If you have no goal, mark one with two piles of clothing.

Place the ball between 10 and 15 yards from the goal line. The distance will depend upon individual boy's kicking strengths. Each boy, in turn, will advance and kick the stationary ball at the goal. If the goalkeeper does not save the ball, it is the kicker's responsibility to run (even if he scores), fetch the ball and return it to you so that you can place it for the next boy to have a shot at the goal. Having shot, and returned the ball, the kicker rejoins the line at the rear.

Stress keeping the ball low. Run through this exercise a few times and change sides for the same practice with the opposite foot.

EXERCISE 28—Part One (LEVEL 2)

Requirements: Boys lined up as in Exercise 27. Pool of balls at position one (see diagram above).

As the boys run, one at a time, slowly roll a ball into their path. Tell them to kick the ball first time. Increase the speed of delivery as they improve.

Stress to your boys that they must meet the ball. Change sides for opposite foot practice.

Once again, each boy is responsible for the ball he kicks. If it goes astray he must fetch it and return it to the ball pool. To rejoin his line he must go around the practice, not across it (see diagram). If this rule is carried out fully it will enable you to have an interrupted practice instead of a stop-start practice.

Try to maintain a fairly constant service to your shooters.

EXERCISE 28—Part Two (LEVEL 3)

This exercise is very similar to the previous one with the exception that you bounce the ball towards your boys instead of rolling it. Once again they must kick the ball first time. A bouncing ball can be difficult to adjust to, so encourage them to shoot and not to worry if they miss the goal. Their accuracy will improve with practice.

Stress getting over the ball. If your boys get underneath a rising ball they will only succeed in kicking it even higher.

Bounce the ball gently to begin with. Increase the height of the bounce gradually.

Change sides for opposite foot practice.

EXERCISE 28—Part Three (LEVEL 3)

As your boys run in turns toward the goal, throw a ball into the air. The ball must drop so as to coincide with the boy's run for him to connect with it first time. The boy has to adjust to the ball and he can either volley it with his feet or head it at the goal. If a boy elects to head the ball, stress to him the importance of heading it downwards and to the corners of the goal.

EXERCISE 28—Part Four (LEVEL 3)

Once again your boys will run singly toward the goal. Your

service to them will vary as for this exercise you will combine the service of the three previous parts of Exercise 28.

Change sides for opposite foot practice.

Part four should easily last for an entire practice session or it can be broken up and used separately. Once again it is up to the coach.

Volleying a ball means kicking it while it is in the air. If a player wants to volley the ball out of danger he should place his kicking foot partially underneath the ball and lean his body back on contact. To keep the ball low he should lean forward when ever possible and keep his head and knee over the ball on contact

Half-volleying is playing the ball as it hits the ground. Once again lean back if you want the ball to rise and get over the ball if you want the ball to stay low.

EXERCISE 29 (LEVEL 3)

Requirements: Divide group into two teams. One ball.

This is a simple game designed for shooting practice. All the play is confined to a penalty area. Place your goalkeeper in goal. (Both goalkeepers could be used at the same time for this game.)

Spread the two teams around the penalty area. The idea is for both teams to score goals by shooting at the same goal.* The goalkeeper starts the game by kicking the ball, high into the air, anywhere inside the penalty area. The ball is then in play and normal soccer rules apply, except offside. As the area will be crowded, encourage first time shooting. The first team to score 10 goals is the winner. If the ball goes out of the penalty area restart the game with a throw-in (even on the goal line). When a goal has been scored the goalkeeper restarts the game by kicking the ball into the air.

Although this is a shooting practice, look for other skills. Tackling and heading will be particularly noticeable and easy to encourage.

*Both teams attack and both teams defend. When team A has the ball, team B tries to obtain it and score, and vice versa.

In all of these shooting practices, impress on your boys that they must follow the ball in after they have shot. The goalkeeper may drop the ball, or it may hit a post and rebound back to them. No one knows for sure how a shot will turn out. Persevere in following-up. A player could follow-up nine shots unsuccessfully. On the 10th shot, which he fails to follow-up, the goalkeeper could drop the ball. A large percentage of goals in soccer are scored from knockdowns and rebounds.

EXERCISE 30 (LEVEL 3)

Requirements: Boys lined up as shown in shooting diagram. Pool of balls at position 2. (See diagram page 59.)

Place your goalkeeper in goal. Position yourself and the balls at the ball pool No. 2, as shown in the diagram.

Roll a ball to the first boy so that he can try to score. He can take the ball on and shoot or he can try to dribble around the goalkeeper. Each boy goes in turn against the goalkeeper.

This is excellent practice for your goalkeeper(s). Encourage him to advance and narrow the angle. Change your goalkeeper periodically to give him a break and another boy an opportunity to practice.

EXERCISE 31 (LEVEL 3)

Requirements: The same as in Exercise 30.

Add one defender to the previous exercise. Place him on the edge of the penalty area in between the goalkeeper and the attackers. In turn each boy attacks the goal and the defender attempts to stop him. Once the defender kicks an attacker's ball away out of his immediate control the next attacker will receive a ball and attack the goal. This stops boys chasing all over the field. Let the defender go right through the line of boys before you replace him with another defender.

Once again this is good practice for the goalkeeper as he must constantly readjust his angle.

Your boys will have opportunities for shooting during practice and competitive games. Goals are the end-product of soccer and shooting is the main method of putting the ball into the back of the net. For this reason I recommend that you have a 10-minute shooting session every time your team practices or as often as possible after your boys have learned and practiced the basic skills.

Throw-ins

Throw-in for accuracy

Throw-in for distance

When a ball goes out of bounds over the touch-lines the game is restarted with a throw-in against the team that last touched the ball. The throw must be taken from the point where the ball crossed the line on its way out of bounds. The thrower must place both hands, preferably at the back of the ball and must throw it from behind or over his head. He must face the field of players with parts of both feet either on or behind the touch line. He cannot play the ball again until it has been touched by another player. A goal cannot be scored directly from a throw-in.

If the player lifts a foot or just drops the ball over his head instead of throwing it, it is deemed a foul throw and the throw-in goes to the other team.

The diagram (page 63) shows a short throw-in which is mainly used for the kind of accuracy required in Diagram 4 of of Set Plays. Note the feet close together and the bent knees.

The diagram below also shows a long throw-in which, though used for distance throwing, can also be very accurate. Note how one leg is in front of the other, which is completely different from the short throw stance. The long throw-in is becoming an increasingly dangerous weapon in modern soccer.

Some players use what is generally considered the short throw-in method to throw the ball considerable distances.

EXERCISE 32—Short Throw-Ins (LEVEL 1)

Requirements: Boys in pairs, three to five yards apart depending upon the strength of their throws. One ball per pair. (Line Method)

In their pairs your boys practice throwing the ball back and forth using the short throw-in method. Stress the importance of keeping parts of both feet on the ground when they throw the ball and the importance of throwing the ball from behind and over their heads.

EXERCISE 33—Long Throw-Ins (LEVEL 1)

Requirements: Boys in pairs, five or more yards apart depending upon the strength of their throws. One ball per pair. (Line Method)

In their pairs your boys practice throwing the ball back and forth using the long throw-in method. Once again stress to your boys the importance of keeping parts of both feet on the ground and throwing the ball over their heads

The skills listed above are probably 85% of the skills needed for a competent soccer player, *at any level.* Teach these skills and you will have laid a solid foundation for your boys to build upon.

Once the skills have been learned, work further with the control practices by varying the service. Have the server serve the ball to the side of his partner, in front of him, and over his head so that he can learn to control a ball which has not been directly thrown at his body.

Since perfect passes are the exception and not the rule, this is an excellent way to practice. The quicker a ball can be controlled the quicker it can be used to advantage.

Instep Kicking	Sole of the Foot Control
Inside of the Foot Pass	Inside of the Foot Control
Heading	Dribbling
Tackling	Shooting Ability

Novice Schedule (Ten Sessions)

This schedule has been prepared to introduce the novice coach and his team to the basic soccer skills. The schedule is laid out in 10 one-hour sessions which can be used twice weekly, or stretched over a period of 10 weeks.

Should you begin practicing three or four weeks before your season starts, you will be partially through the schedule when your first league game has to be played. If, during the pre-season period, you have also fitted in a few practice games against other novice teams, you and your boys will have had an introduction to soccer, however brief, and will have an idea of what the game is all about.

GAMES: When playing scrimmage games:

• Stop the play to make a coaching point or to explain a rule, but don't do so continuously. Let the boys play. Continuously stopping the play ruins the game for them.

• At first don't worry about the offside rule. The problem probably won't arise to begin with anyway.* Explain the rule to them and begin to apply it at about the fourth or fifth scrim-

(*Most novice teams usually hold players back near their goal line or at least near the edge of their penalty area. This makes it very difficult for players to run into offside positions.)

mage game. By this time they will be able to appreciate the significance of the rule without understanding the details. These take time to learn. See offside section, pages 123 to 130. See also page 113.

● Relate to a recently finished practice during the immediate scrimmage game. If your boys have just been practicing the sole of the foot control, for instance, encourage them to control the ball in this manner whenever possible.

When these sessions have been completed, you and your boys will have been through a crash course in basic soccer. You will also have seen how an effective coaching session can be worked out. It will then be up to you to work out your own sessions. When you do, use the suggested practices (there are 33 of them in this book), and begin to introduce ideas of your own.

You will find that a 10- to 15-minute warmup including things like dribbling and juggling will help loosen up your boys before their practice sessions.

SESSION 1

Scrimmage Game, 15 minutes. Divide your squad into two teams and play a scrimmage game. Coats or balls will suffice for goals if you do not have a soccer field. If you only have a small group, make goals on the touchlines and play across the field to save your boys running the full length and tiring themselves unduly. This scrimmage will give you an opportunity to explain the basic rules of soccer to your boys (handball, out of bounds calls, etc.) while giving them a chance to play a game immediately.

Instep Kicking Practice, 20 minutes. Use Exercise 1. Explain the basic principles.

Short Throw-In Practice, 10 minutes. Use Exercise 32.

Scrimmage Game, 15 minutes. Continue to explain the basic rules.

SESSION 2

Instep Kicking Practice, 20 minutes. Use Exercise 1. Reaffirm basic principles.

Heading Practice, 20 minutes. Use Exercise 8. Explain the principles of where, why and how to head the ball.

Scrimmage Game, 20 minutes. Continue to explain the basic rules.

SESSION 3

Instep Kicking Practice, 10 minutes. Use Exercise 1. (As well as being a necessary practice, Exercise 1 is a good warming up session.)

Heading Practice, 10 minutes. Use Exercise 8. Reaffirm basic principles.

Inside of the Foot Passing Practice, 20 minutes. Use Exercise 3.

Scrimmage Game, 20 minutes. Briefly mention positions, their functions and purposes.

SESSION 4

Instep Kicking Practice, 10 minutes. Use Exercise 1. Your boys should by now be beginning to grasp and apply the basic principles of instep kicking. Keep stressing these principles.

Inside of the Foot Passing Practices, 10 minutes. Use Exercise 3. Reaffirm the basic principles.

Dribbling Practice, 20 minutes. Use Exercise 11. Explain the basic principles, stressing to your boys that they must keep the ball in front of and fairly close to them.

Scrimmage Game, 20 minutes. Begin to place your boys into positions.

SESSION 5

Instep Kicking Practice, 10 minutes. Use Exercise 1.

Dribbling Practice, 10 minutes. Use Exercise 11. Reaffirm the basic principles.

Controls Practice, 20 minutes. All of the suggested practices for basic controls are very similar in execution.

- Sole of the foot control, 10 minutes. Use Exercise 15.
- Inside of the foot control, 20 minutes. Use Exercise 17.
- Explain the basic principles of both controls.

Scrimmage Game, 20 minutes.   Continue to place your boys into positions. Also, keep explaining the laws of the game. By now you should have introduced your boys to the offside rule. See the discussion of offside following session 10.

SESSION 6

Controls Practice, 20 minutes.
- Sole of the foot control, 5 minutes. Use Exercise 15.
- Inside of the foot control, 5 minutes. Use Exercise 17.
- Instep control, 10 minutes. Use Exercise 19.

Tackling Practice, 20 minutes. Use Exercise 22. Stress the basic principles.

Scrimmage Game, 20 minutes. Continue positioning your boys. By now they should be starting to understand a little more about positions and their functions.

SESSION 7

Instep Kicking Practices, 10 minutes. Use Exercise 1.

Tackling Practice, 10 minutes. Use Exercise 22. Stress the basic principles.

Controls Practice, 20 minutes.
- Thigh control, 10 minutes. Use Exercise 20.
- Chest control, 10 minutes. Use Exercise 21.

The above are advanced skills. If you would prefer, practice sole of the foot and inside of the foot controls exercises 15 and 17.

Scrimmage Game, 20 minutes. By now your boys should be playing their positions with a little bit of knowledge. Keep explaining their functions to them. Continue to explain the laws of the game.

SESSION 8

Instep Kicking Practice, 10 minutes. Use Exercise 1. If your boys have improved at Exercise 1, advance to Exercise 2.

Long Throw-in Practice, 10 minutes. Explain the basic principles of the long throw-in. Compare and contrast it with the short throw-in.

Goal-keeping Practice, 20 minutes.   Use Exercise 25 (all parts).

Scrimmage Game, 20 minutes.   Continue talking to your boys about their positions and the laws of the game.

SESSION 9

Instep Kicking Practice, 10 minutes.   Use Exercise 1 or 2. Reaffirm basic principles.

Dribbling Practice, 10 minutes.   Use Exercise 11. If your boys have improved at Exercise 11, advance to Exercise 12.

Shooting Practice, 20 minutes.   Use Exercise 27. The instep kick will be used in this practice so continue to stress basic principles. Also stress keeping the ball low.

Scrimmage Game, 20 minutes.   Continue with positional placement.

SESSION 10

Shooting Practice, 20 minutes.   Start at Exercise 27 and advance to Exercise 28, part 1.

Skills Session, 20 minutes.   Ask for the greatest number of consecutive heads, singly or in pairs. Time your boys' dribbling speed over a set distance or around a few stakes. See page 70.

Scrimmage Game, 20 minutes.   Before the game, explain once again what is expected of each boy in his position.

The more scrimmage games that can be arranged against other teams, the better for your boys.

When explaining the offside rule, don't go into too much detail. Simply tell your boys to try to have two opponents between them and their opponent's goal-line when they are in the opponent's half of the field, and to try not to get ahead of the ball.

Also explain that they cannot be offside in their own half of the field, nor directly from corner-kicks and throw-ins.

Performance Graph

As I have already mentioned, it is a good idea to have a regular skills session. For this purpose I have designed a very basic program which should take less than 20 minutes per team. These sessions can be held whenever you desire, but I recommend that you hold them fairly regularly.

More skills can be added to those already described. At first your boys will improve their scores by leaps and bounds. After a period their scores will level off and they will find it difficult to improve further (especially the dribbling). When this happens, move on to another practice, returning to the performance graph at a later date or even another season.

If you decide against using this graph, still encourage your boys to practice these skills, either by themselves or with you. This could be a good warming-up session.

The graph in itself does not tell you anything about a boy's ability other than his scores and his improvement at certain skills.

Apart from seeing which boys obtained the best scores it is also interesting to see which boys made the greatest improvements.

Consecutive heads

Divide your boys into two's, three's or four's, depending upon the number of balls available to your team. A ball between two would be ideal. Each boy, in turn, sees how many times he can head the ball before it touches the ground. Each boy begins the practice by throwing the ball onto his head. Allow five minutes for this skill in order to give your boys plenty of attempts. Each boy counts his partner's score. Write in the highest number at the end of the exercise.

Consecutive controls (Juggling)

Repeat the previous exercise reading control for heads. (Obviously the use of hands or arms will not count.)

Dribbling (Slalom)

Requirements—four to six stakes. One ball.

Place your stakes, three long strides apart, in a straight line.

Name:								Best Score
Consecutive Heads								
Consecutive Controls								
Dribbling (Slalom)								

Use the same exercise as laid out in exercise 12. Time and record each boy on only one run, having allowed him one practice attempt.

If a boy leaves out a stake add one second to his time. Also add one second if he hits a stake.

If you start this exercise with four stakes, continue to use four stakes throughout.

Working on a rotation basis, all three skills could be run at the same time. Simply divide your team into three groups. When the jugglers have completed juggling, they move on to consecutive heading, the headers moving on to dribbling and the dribblers moving on to juggling. Two rotations and you are finished. You, as coach, must stay with the dribbling group to time them. Help from an assistant or assistants will reduce your burden.

At the end of the session, note each boy's performances under the appropriate headings (you can fill in the dribbling as you time it.) I suggest that you keep each boy's graph instead of expecting him to bring it along regularly.

PART THREE

PLAYING THE GAME

Basic Outline of the Rules

The game of soccer is divided into two periods. (Check with your local association on this point—many associations play by quarters.) At half-time the interval of rest is normally five to 10 minutes.

Before each game the team captains flip a coin. The teams winning the call can elect to defend either goal or to kick off from the center spot.

If the team winning the call chooses the kick-off, the other team has the choice of ends. If team A elects to kick off the first half, team B will kick at the start of the second half. At the half, the teams change over and defend the goal they were attacking. After each goal, the team scored on re-starts the game from the center-spot. From a kick-off, the ball must be played the distance of its own circumference (27"-28") into the opponent's half before it is considered in play.

When winning a call, the captain should take the conditions into consideration. The wind may blow out at half-time. The sun may be going down. Conditions change. Try to use the call to your team's advantage.

Soccer is a very fluid game in which each team progresses, mainly by a series of kicks, towards the other team's goal. The ball can be played by any part of the body excepting the hands or the arms (see Law XII[i], page 114). The one exception to this rule is the goalkeeper, who can handle the ball provided he is in his own penalty area. Once outside his penalty area he is subject to the same rules as the outfield players. All free-kicks given for handball are direct, that is, a goal can be scored directly from the spot where the offense occurred. Handball in the penalty area is also a direct kick but it differs slightly by being taken from the penalty spot. Indirect free-kicks must be touched by another player of either side, before a goal can be scored (see Law XIII, page 117). All defending players must be 10 yards away from the ball when a free-kick has been awarded against them unless, for example, the ball is eight yards from the goal-line and the defenders are standing on the goal-line between the goal-posts. In this case the defenders are permitted to stand on the goal-line as otherwise they would be off the field of play. A referee signals for an indirect free-kick by raising his arm. No signal is given for a direct free-kick.

A penalty-kick (see Law XIV) can be awarded for fouls anywhere inside the penalty area—irrespective of the position of the ball—as well as for handball. There are nine offenses for which a penalty kick is the punishment (see Law XII, page 114). Time can be added onto a game, at the end of either half, to allow for a penalty-kick to be taken. These kicks really hurt in soccer as the kicker has a free shot at the defending goalkeeper from the penalty spot, which is only 12 yards from the goal-line. The goalkeeper must stand on his goal-line until the ball is kicked and all the other players must stand outside of the penalty area but inside the field of play (see diagram, page 95).

BALL IN AND OUT OF PLAY

To be out of bounds a ball must completely cross over the goal-line or touch-line (see Law IX[a]). Out of bounds applies to goal-kicks, corner-kicks, throw-ins and goals, or when the game has been stopped by the referee (see Law IX[b]). When the ball goes out of bounds (except when a goal has been scored or the referee stops the game) the game is restarted by a throw-in or a kick being awarded against the team who last touched the ball. If team A played the ball over the touch-lines the throw-in will be awarded to team B and vice versa. If the ball goes out of bounds over the goal-line, the game is restarted by either a corner-kick or a goal-kick, depending upon which team last played the ball. If the defending team last played the ball, it is a corner-kick to the attacking team; if the attacking team last played the ball it is a goal-kick to the defending team (see diagram page 91).

The game can be stopped at certain times when neither side is guilty of an infringement, if, for example, two boys collide and are injured or the ball bursts. In such situations the game is restarted by a bounce-up or drop-ball, usually between two players of opposing teams, at the spot where the ball was when the game was stopped (see Law VIII). When a ball is dropped for a bounce-up it cannot be played until it touches the ground.

Charging an opponent, shoulder to shoulder, is permissable within the framework of the rules when the ball is within playing distance.

In soccer there is an "advantage clause" which the referee can apply at his discretion. He would apply the clause if a defender fouls an attacker but the ball breaks to another attacker, who has a good chance of scoring a goal. It may be a foul, but to award it would be to penalize the team which has been offended against.

This is why you should impress upon your boys that they must always play to the whistle. A foul may be committed, but until the whistle is blown and the referee awards a foul, it is not considered a foul.

Time can be added on for injuries or other causes and the amount of additional time is left to the discretion of the referee. Other than this there are no time outs in soccer. (Once again, check with your local association on this point.)

At kick-offs, free-kicks, penalty-kicks and corner-kicks, the ball must travel the distance of its own circumference before it can be considered in play. A goal-kick must travel out of the penalty area before it can be played (see Law XVI, page 121).

Kick-offs, throw-ins, free-kicks, corners, penalties and goal-kicks can only be played once by the taker. Before the taker can touch the ball again, another player, of either side, has to play the ball.

The most difficult rule to understand in soccer is the off-side rule (see Law XI, page 113). Read Law XI thoroughly, the operative words being "at the moment the ball is played."

The maximum number of players on a soccer team is 11, one of whom is the goalkeeper (see Law III).

A player must not wear any equipment which can be dangerous to other players, such as a watch, a ring, or dangerously cleated boots. (See Law IV, page 105, and also check with your cal association on what boots and cleats they allow to be worn.)

The team at the end of the game with the greatest number of goals is the winner. If both teams have the same number—cup games and play-off games excepting—the result will be a tie. (Remember, the ball must completely cross the goal-line for a goal to be scored.) See Law X, page 112.)

The complete laws of the game are in the Appendix. They are reproduced by the kind permission of FIFA.

Equipment

A player must not wear anything which could be dangerous to another player. (See Law IV, page 105.)

A player's equipment consists of:

One pair of boots: Most associations are wary of plastic- or nylon-studded boots so check with them. The majority of American boys play in rubber-studded/cleated boots.

One pair of socks: Full length.

One pair of shin-guards: A sensible precaution.

One jock-strap: For support and safety.

One pair of shorts: Not too tight. In many cases, the baggier the better. This sounds peculiar to most Americans, but baggy shorts give freedom of movement whereas tight shorts are restrictive.

One shirt: Preferably long sleeved as this offers protection to players if they fall. Goalkeepers should always wear long sleeved jerseys.

Pads: Players can wear knee pads and elbow pads. Goalkeepers often do. They can be a sensible precaution although they may prove to be troublesome and restrictive.

Don't be afraid to play while wearing glasses. I suggest plastic frames with a band at the back of the head attached to the frame so that if they are hit they remain on the head. The obvious problem one thinks of with glasses is heading the ball. The secret is to keep one's eyes on the ball until impact.

Restarts

Kick-Off. Kick-offs start both halves, and restart the game after a goal has been scored. They are taken from the center spot.

Penalty-Kick. Penalty-kicks are taken from one of the two penalty spots.

Corner-Kick (C.K.). Corner-kicks are taken from one of the four corner areas depending upon where the defending team kicked the ball out of bounds along the goal-line. If the ball went out of bounds nearest to the left corner flag, the corner-

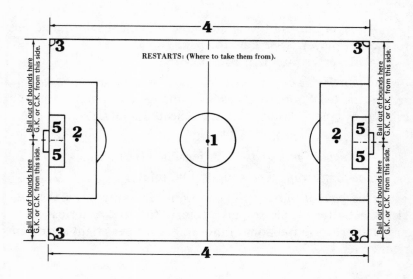

kick is taken from the left. The imaginary center of the cross-bar, as shown on both goals, can be used as the determining factor when deciding these calls.

Throw-In. The throw-in is the method of restarting the game when the ball goes out of bounds anywhere along either touch-line. The throw is taken from the point where the ball crossed the touch-line while going out of bounds.

Goal-Kick (G.K.). Use the same method as used for corner-kicks to determine which side the goal-kick should be taken from. A goal-kick can be taken from anywhere inside that half of the goal area, on the side nearest to where the ball went out of bounds. It does not have to be placed exactly on the corner of the goal area, although it may be. Many times the corner of the goal area has a hole where it has been over-used. This hole is a disadvantage to the team playing the ball.

Bounce-Up. Restarts play anywhere on the field where play was stopped by the referee when neither team was guilty of an infringement.

Hints on Positioning Players

Here are brief explanations of each position's requirement. These requirements or guidelines are only general and are offered to help the novice coach over the initial teething period. As the season progresses he will find out more exactly his wants and needs and he can advance from there.

Goalkeepers:

See page 53 for the explanation on goalkeeping, which lists the basic requirements needed by a goalkeeper.

Fullbacks:

Try to play your best tackler at fullback. This is not always possible or even necessary, but try to apply it as a general rule. A fullback should be firm and positive in the tackle and quick to recover if he is beaten. He must also be able to kick a soccer ball a good distance and with a reasonable degree of accuracy.

Of the four fullbacks, which most teams play, the two center backs need to work closely with each other. They also need to be above average in their heading ability.

The two wide and flank fullbacks need be neither wonderful headers of a soccer ball nor large in physique. An ideal player for this position is a small, wiry, terrier-like player who hustles and is quick into the tackle. Fullbacks should be good markers of opponents. This means they must be able to pick up an opponent whenever the situation demands.

Linkmen:

The linkman is the connector of a soccer team. He joins defense and attack together and his job includes both defensive and attacking responsibilities. A linkman is in the game almost continuously, whether by direct involvement or by running into defensive or attacking positions. Therefore, he needs to be a good worker and a good runner so that he can keep in contact with the play. He also needs to win the ball in tackles, regularly.

A linkman needs to be able to pass a ball accurately and to support his attack while always being prepared to go through and have a shot at goal. And, once an attack has broken down, he must be prepared to run back and help defend his goal. It's hard work. The linkman is the workhorse of the team. Like a fullback, a linkman needs to be able to pick up opponents as his primary job is defense. In today's soccer a linkman is primarily a defender who attacks when he is sure of his defense.

Strikers:

A striker's main job is very simple, to score goals. He must always be alert to any scoring possibilities, no matter how small. This means running after a ball which appears to be going out of play or chasing and challenging for a ball which an opponent has under control. In short, a striker must hustle and try to make defenders nervous; nervous defenders make mistakes.

A striker should be able to finish off successfully a good percentage of goal chances with either his head or his feet. And he should be quick to sense or see any possible opportunities before they happen. Ball control is another requirement for a striker since he often receives a ball in close situations where there is no support at hand. In such situations he either has to wait for help to arrive or go it alone. In either case his ball control will be called into full play.

If possible, select your strikers to complement each other and work as a unit. For example, a small ball playing striker who regularly scores goals would the be ideal partner for a big, awkward, hustling striker who is good in the air. Strikers must learn to feed off one another.

Wingers:

A winger is a striker who plays on the flanks. He may or may not score as many goals as the central striker, but his main job is to supply a service of the ball to them. Therefore, he should be a good and accurate kicker as he has to play the ball to his teammates often in a crowded goal-mouth.

A winger who is fast and an accurate kicker can be a very devastating player and a great addition to his team.

The most dangerous ball in soccer is the "pull-back." This is a ball which has been taken to the goal line and then passed back across the face of the goal. It is a dangerous pass because players of both teams are forced to meet it, the attacker to try and score and the defender to relieve the situation. For this reason many own-goals are scored by defenders because they are facing their own goal and a hard hit pull-back ball confuses them. Forwards love this situation, for they're running in to meet a ball, which, if it comes to them, will give them an excellent chance of scoring.

GENERAL TIPS

Team Balance. Balance your team by placing left-footed players on the left side of the team and right-footed players on right side. The latter should cause no problems, the former might. (This does not mean, however, that a left-footed player cannot play as a right winger.)

Spread out. Your boys will tend to bunch at first. Attempt to spread them out intelligently, to cover as much of an area as possible without exposing your defense. To achieve a good balance between spreading and bunching takes time, patience, and a fair amount of frustration.

The diagram on page 80 shows a soccer field which has been divided into thirds so as to show the approximate areas where the respective parts of the team will do the majority of their work. It is a very rough guideline for coaches to work on.

Although soccer is a fluid game, and not rigid, it is good to

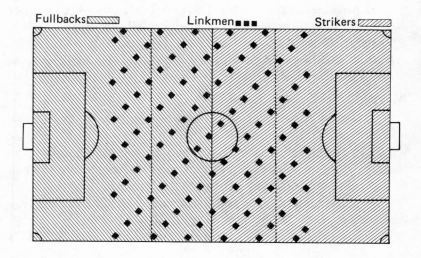

show this diagram to your boys so that they can see approximately where they should be on the field of play.

Notice how each third is over-lapped by the adjoining third. This is to show how each part of the team should be joining and working together as well as to show boys that they are not restricted to set areas. A fullback can score goals and a striker can be called upon to defend.

Basic Formations and Tactics

Boys who have just been introduced to soccer, especially younger boys, are difficult, if not impossible, to discipline into holding their positions. The notable exception is the goalkeeper—sometimes he holds his position too much.

Beginners also have a tendency to follow the ball and thus to bunch. This can be called a good fault (if such a thing exists) insofar as it shows their eagerness to participate. Don't worry! The main objectives for novices should be to play with a soccer ball in competition or alone, and to enjoy themselves. Later on, when they have learned a little about this wonderful game, they can learn about positions. I'm not advocating that your boys should be allowed to chase the ball all over the field. I'm just preparing you for that probability.

BASIC FORMATIONS

A soccer team consists of 11 players and the formations they play are numerous. In this section you will see three of the most used modern formations, plus their forerunner, the W-M, along with a summary of their functions.

In soccer we start from the back when translating formations, therefore 4-2-4 means, four fullbacks, two linkmen, and four forwards. We assume that each team has a goalkeeper so we don't mention him, numbering only the outfield players.

W-M

The formation in vogue when I learned to play soccer was the W-M formation. It is a sound system which is still in use. The W-M is the daddy of all modern systems with the emphasis on midfield.

The W-M formation uses five attacking players. Two are wingers, who attack down the flanks; two are inside forwards, one of whom drops behind to support and feed his main goal-

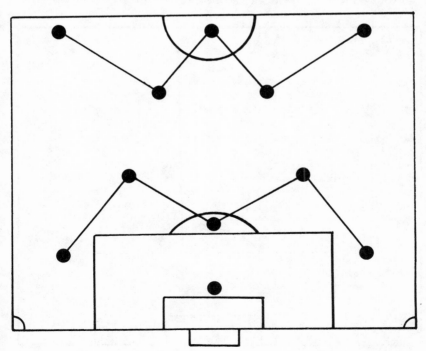

scorers; and one is the out and out spearhead, the center-forward. The forwards attack almost exclusively, as they have few defensive responsibilities.

This system uses five defending players. Two are fullbacks who play wide to combat their opposing wingers; one is the center half, who plays in the middle of the defense; and two are wing halves, one of whom is the more defensive of the two. He usually stays in a defensive position, thus allowing the other wing-half to push forward and support his forwards.

Today's formations demand that everyone goes forward and everyone goes back as the situation dictates. Players are becoming more and more interchangeable. This means that a full-back who moves into a forward position, however briefly, becomes a forward and is expected to be reasonably competent in the position while he holds it. Defenders are forced to support (help) their forwards more today: as teams become more defensively-minded, forwards cannot penetrate and score as many goals as they once did. This is why defenders are scoring more goals than ever before.

By the same token, forwards today have defensive responsibilities which they seldom had before.

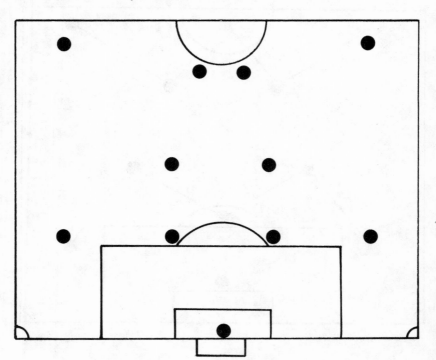

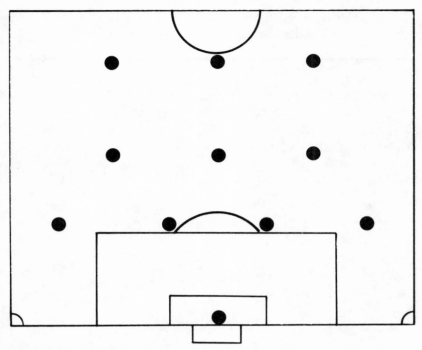

4-2-4 (At left)

This is an attacking formation. The four strikers, two of whom stay wide and are also called wingers, play in the attack.

The two linkmen in the center of the 4-2-4 are both attackers and defenders. When your team has the ball they are attackers; when the opposition has the ball they are defenders. They should be always conscious of their defensive position and sure that they can return to it quickly if their team loses the ball.

The back four players are primarily defenders. The two fullbacks can attack down their flanks at certain times when the flow of the game demands it. The two center backs are very limited. in this respect and are used, almost exclusively, for defensive purposes.

The 4-2-4 and the W-M formations are quite similar.

4-3-3 (Above)

This is a more defensive formation than 4-2-4. The play is built up mainly from the three linkmen. The three strikers have more space to cover but when on the attack they expect support from at least one of the linkmen or midfield players. (See the support positions of the linkmen in the diagram on page 96.)

In defense, 4-3-3 is very similar to 4-2-4 except for greater depth. The fullbacks can still play an adventuresome role.

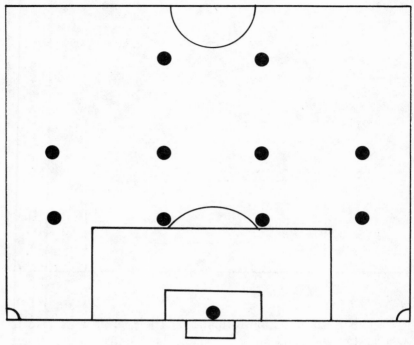

4-4-2

This is a defensive system whereby a team plays four linkmen across the field in front of the back four. It is a frustrating system to play against, for it denies a team space in the center of the field and on the flanks.

The two front men tend to become isolated and must learn to feed off of one another. Theirs is a hard job and when they receive the ball they generally have to delay play, by holding the ball, until support can reach them.

4-4-2 demands that men support the front two strikers by quickly joining the attack from the back. The two wide fullbacks will still be able to link with the attack.

Positional Terms: then and now

Soccer terms have changed considerably in the last decade and a half, as have formations and systems of play. Comparing the positional terms as used in the W-M formation with the terms of the modern mode systems shows us much.

W-M Formation Terms:

G.K.—Goalkeeper

R.F.B.—Right Fullback or right back.

R.H.—Right Half or Right Halfback or Right Wing Half

C.H.B.—Center Halfback or Center Half or Center Fullback or Center Back

L.H.—Left Half or Left Halfback or Left Wing Half.

L.F.B.—Left Fullback or Left Back.

O.R.—Outside Right or Right Wing or Right Flankman

I.R.—Inside Right or Right Inside Forward

C.F.—Center Forward

I.L.—Inside Left or Left Inside Forward

O.L.—Outside Left or Left Wing or Left Flankman

From these basic positions we had groupings, other than defense and attack. The Right Half, Center Half and Left Half were called the Halfback Line. The Inside Right, Center Forward and Inside Left were called Inside Forwards. The Outside Right and the Outside Left were called Wingers. The Right Half and the Left Half were called Wing Halves while the Right and Left Backs were referred to as the Fullbacks.

More Modern Terms:

G.K.—Goalkeeper or Goaltender

R.F.B.—Right Fullback. As before.

R.C.F.B.—Right Center Fullback.

L.C.F.B.—Left Center Fullback.

L.F.B.—Left Fullback. As before.

L.M.—Linkmen. Any player who plays in midfield and performs a fetch and carry role is called a linkman, whether right, left or center, etc.

Strikers—All forwards are now referred to as Strikers whether right, left or center, etc.

C.F.—The term Center Forward is still used widely to describe the Central Striker or the Spearhead of the attack. As before.

Wingers—The term Winger is still in popular use although most teams only play one Winger, through necessity rather than desire.

Today's terminology seems simple and straightforward compared with previous terminology. This is because three terms can be used to describe all of the outfield positions: Fullback, Linkman and Striker. The game has become more tactically minded, faster, more competitive, and possibly (as some people think) more stereotyped and less entertaining. The players, however, still perform the same skills with the same aim of scoring more goals than the opposition. Don't let terms confuse you, for soccer is basically the most simple of games. "It is made difficult by players and coaches."

Tactics:

To begin with don't concern yourself with them. Tactics are only important when everyone understands his job on the field. That may take a long time. Your main job as a coach is to make sure that your boys learn to play with and to use their soccer skills. Tactics can be introduced at a later stage; in my opinion, the later the better. I feel that skill and individual flair are the first things that should be taught and encouraged in young boys. When the major skills are well learned, you can gradually introduce tactics. Don't burden your boys down with too much, too soon.

Many people have said that in today's game of soccer there are too many tactics. I agree! Tactics are in the mind. If you think a system is defensive you'll play it defensively. No system is completely defensive or attacking, it has to have elements of both aspects of the game. As such, any system becomes whatever is made of it.

When selecting a system of play for your team, suit the system to the players, not the players to the system. Remember an old soccer cliche: "Attack is the best form of defense."

The Pivot System

The pivot-system is designed for defensive covering. It is a fairly easy system to put into operation. It enables defenders to challenge for the ball with the knowledge that they are supported by a covering colleague. A team which uses the pivot-system has depth in defense and cannot easily be beaten by one pass as a square or flat defense can be.

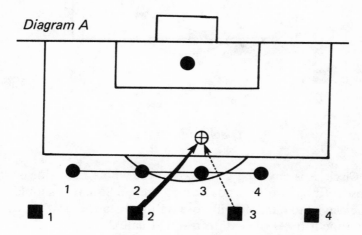

Diagram A

Diagram A shows team Circle caught square across the length of their own penalty area. This gives attacker Square 2 the fairly easy task of playing the ball behind defense Circle to give Square 3, who has timed his run correctly, (see Law XI, offside) an excellent change of scoring. One pass has beaten an entire defense.

Diagram B shows attack Square in position similar to the one as shown in diagram A. Defense Circle are, however, in a far superior position this time because they are using the pivot-system (pivoting on Circle 2) and have, therefore, a great deal of cover. Now a ball played through defense Circle will cause little trouble, if any, provided the defense is well drilled. We will now examine diagrams B and C (on page 88).

Diagram B:

Circle 1 is in a covering position for Circle 2 who is engaging Square 2.

Circle 2 is engaging Square 2, the man on the ball. Notice how he is showing Square 2 the space to his right. He is trying to channel Square's attack away from the goal and to the flank where its alternatives can be restricted. The defense is pivoting on him. Should he be beaten by Square 2 both Circle 1 and Circle 3 can come to his assistance.

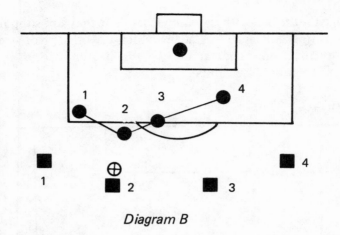

Diagram B

Circle 3 is covering Circle 2 and the whole right side of the defense. He is also in a position to engage Square 3 should the ball be played to him. He will close up the distance between them in the time it takes the ball to travel Square 3.

Circle 4 is covering the entire defense. He has given his winger, Square 4, the freedom of team Circle's left flank so that he can guard the immediate danger. Although his winger has a great deal of space, it is difficult to exploit. Should the ball be played across the field to Square 4, Circle 4 would engage him while Circle 3 would provide the cover.

Circle 4 should be positioned so that he can see the developing play, and also his winger, to insure that he doesn't sneak across or behind him unexpectedly.

Diagram C

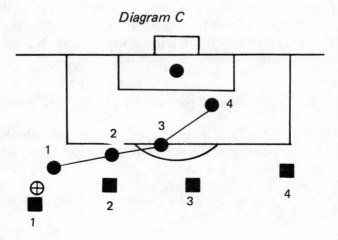

Diagram C:

Circle 1 is engaging Square 1, the man on the ball, who has dropped to receive the ball from Square 2. Circle 1 is trying to force Square 1 down the flank.

Circle 2 is covering Circle 1. He can quickly engage Square 2 should the ball be played to him. (In this instance, Circle 1 would then revert to covering Circle 2 as he is doing in diagram B). Circle 3 is covering the whole right side of the defense. He can engage Square 3 should the ball be played to him.

The two center fullbacks should pivot on one another, in relation to the ball, whenever possible.

If the ball were played to Square 4, in diagram C, the players would simply adjust so that it would appear that, defensively, diagram C had reversed itself. Square 4 would be engaged by Circle 4. Circle 3 would cover Circle 4 while keeping within distance of Square 3. Circle 2 would cover the entire left side of the defense while still being able to engage Square 2 should the ball be played to him. Circle 1 would be covering the entire defense.

It would appear that diagram B had reversed itself, defensively, if the ball were played to Square 3 and the defense adjusted accordingly. Work it out for yourself on a sheet of paper.

Teaching the Pivot-System

A good way to teach your defenders how to use the pivot-system is to play attack versus defense. Your forwards can also benefit from this practice. Place your goalkeeper in goal. Line your four fullbacks up to prepare for a kick-off against them. Your forwards kick off and attack the goal. The attack continues until the defenders either kick the ball over the half-way line or the forwards score a goal. Normal soccer rules apply for this practice, including throw-ins and corner-kicks.

You could well have enough boys to form two or even three, four-man forward lines. Number the separate forward lines from one upwards and send them against the defense in sequence.

During the practice you can coach the pivot-system (as well as any other points that appear.)

On the whistle your boys must "freeze." (Stand exactly where they are.) This enables you to explain to your defenders where they should be in relation to the play.

This is a very enjoyable and useful practice.

Set Plays

Set plays from corners, free-kicks and throw-ins in your opponents' half can set up scoring chances. (Penalty shots are obviously direct shots on the opponent's goal.) Kick-offs, free-kicks, and throw-ins in your half are designed to gain space and to keep possession of the ball, allowing you to advance into attacking positions. The nearer you get to your opponents' goal, the more opposition faces you.

Kick-off to Retain Possession:

Circle 1 kicks off and passes to Circle 2. Circle 2 passes to Circle 3. Circle 3 passes to Circle 1 who has progressed into his opponents' half of the field. Circle 2 and Circle 4 are also available and ready to receive the ball.

By thoughtful soccer, team Circle have retained possession of the ball instead of losing it as they probably would have had Circle 3 blasted the ball upfield. And why give your opponents an early feel of the ball? Better to deny them it. There is the added incentive of the high percentage of goals scored early on

Kick-off

Player ←------- Ball ←——

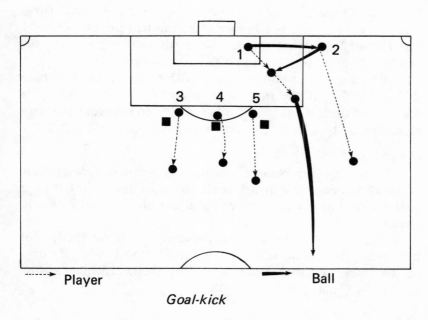

Player →   Ball →

Goal-kick

in games. If you deny the opposition the ball they may well make a mistake on their first kick and present you with a scoring chance.*

Goal-Kick

Goalkeepers find they can cause their team problems if they can't kick the ball very far from goal-kicks. A simple method to aid keepers is known as the short or quick goalkick. The goalkeeper Circle 1 passes the ball to a defender Circle 2 who is well placed to return the ball to him. The keeper can now advance, observing the 4 step rule, and play the ball from near the edge of the penalty area having the extra advantage of being able to kick the ball from his hands.

Notice how Circle 5, Circle 4, and Circle 3 are waiting on

---

*This needs some qualification for beginning teams. This type of kick-off is fine once your boys can perform at a good level. Until they can, though, they may be well advised to give the ball away by kicking it as far into their opponent's half as possible. Controlling the ball is not too important at basic levels. Territorial advantage can be as it keeps the ball away from your goal.

the edge of their penalty area in case their help is needed. However, as soon as the goalkeeper kicks the ball upfield, Circle 1 and Circle 2 run past square's forwards (no further than the half-way line) placing them in offside positions.

You can also let your defender with the strongest kick take the goal-kick. If the opposition places a man on Circle 2 it means that there is one less man in position to intercept the goal-kick. It may be a long time until a man is placed on Circle 2.

Direct Free Kick:

Defending team Square lines up a four-man wall, last man in line with the near post and the ball, to stop a direct shot at their goal. This aids the goalkeeper by giving him a smaller area to protect.

Circle 1 fakes to shoot but passes square across the face of the penalty area giving Circle 2 a shooting opportunity. By passing to Circle 2, Circle 1 has opened up the goal which was restricted by square's defensive wall.

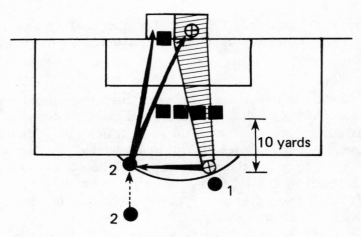

Free-kick

There are many variations on this one theme. They are all concerned with getting a shot at the goal. Learn the basic kick first and the alternatives will come to you.

The more moves involved the greater the possibility of failure. So keep it simple.

Throw In to Retain Possession:

Circle 1 throws the ball to Circle 2 who plays it back to

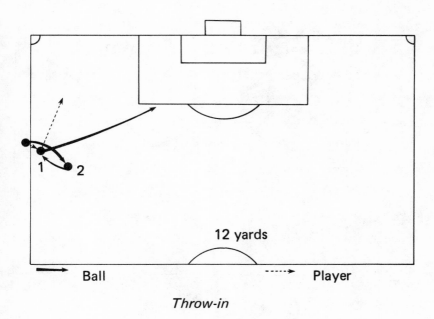

Ball   Player

Throw-in

Circle 1. Team Circle retains possession and Circle 1 can proceed by picking his best move. Circle 1 is advised to throw the ball to Circle 2's head as this guarantees the most reliable return.

This simple, basic play keeps the ball from the other team. It is a set-play which can be used in any part of the field.

Corner Kick:

Many young boys have difficulty in reaching anywhere inside the penalty area when they are taking a corner kick.

To this end, Circle 1 passes to Circle 7 who attempts to cross the ball into the penalty area. Timing is important, for Circle 7 must be able to run onto the ball. Once the timing is perfected this will prove to be a valuable set play as a moving ball is easier to kick for distance than a still one.

Look at the positions of Circle 2 and Circle 3. They are close to the nearest spot to the kicker as this is the defending team's weakest near spot. They are close together because things happen so quickly in tight situations and they feed off one another. The ball may be crossed to Circle 2 and he will attempt to play it across the face of the goal. He will be tightly marked by a defending player and a touch of the ball may be all he can manage. Circle 3 expects something and should Circle 2 get a

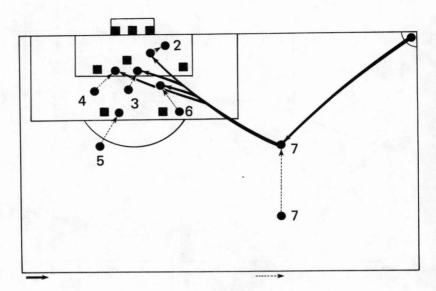

Corner-kick

touch of the ball he is in position to attack the goal. Note how Circle 3 runs from the edge of the six-yard box. He has left himself space to run into as have Circle 2, Circle 4, Circle 5, and Circle 6. Circle 5 and Circle 6 are waiting around the edge of the penalty area for any loose balls that are played out of the danger zone. They are also in position to chase back and defend should the attack break down.

The attack is spread out with players covering the penalty area at strategic points instead of bunching up and getting in each others' way. All of the attacking players are in position to go forward. Circle 1, having taken the corner-kick, should then run into the penalty area on the look-out for any opportunities which could lead to a goal.

If you are lucky enough to have a corner-kicker who can kick the ball accurately into the penalty area in front of the goal, great. Use him to your full advantage, remembering to position your attackers so that they intelligently cover the penalty area. By doing this you'll gain the greatest advantage from his kicks.

You can also try a short corner-kick whereby the kicker quickly passes the ball to a colleague who is very close. Remember, defenders cannot move closer than 10 yards until the ball is played.

Penalty-Kick:

The penalty-kick is the simplest of all the set plays to understand as it is the most basic. It is a 1 vs. 1 situation, loaded, very favorably, on the side of the kicker. (See Basic Outline of the Rules of Soccer, page 73). The most effective kick is a hard shot into any of the four corners of the goal. In general, the lower the shot the better.

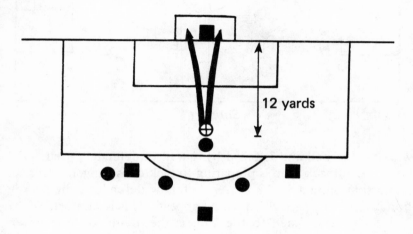

12 yards

Penalty-Kick

Each player will develop his own style of taking penalties. Some will try to place the ball accurately, others will blast it, while some will try to combine accuracy with power. When your boys practice penalty kicking, stress to them the importance of keeping the ball low.

Support (Men to the Ball)

In soccer, "support" or "men to the ball" means teammates helping one another. Support is vital a part of the modern game of soccer. Without it, a team lacks alternatives. A forward

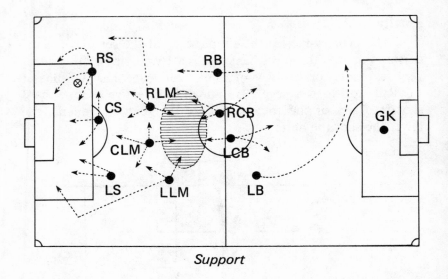

Support

who has the ball and is faced by a wall of defenders needs support. A fullback who is preparing to tackle his winger, needs to know that should he be beaten, a fellow defender is in a position to plug any gap which would appear. This is support.

Support, or men to the ball, is the lifeline of any soccer team.

Support begins from the back of the defense. And here we must not forget the goalkeeper, who can support his defense by constructive shouting. He sees the developing play and can shout helpful information to his teammates. They, in turn, must listen to him and use his advice.

The diagram above shows team Circle on the attack. They are using a 4-3-3 formation.

G.K. Slightly advanced from goal area in case of breakaway by opposing team.

R.B. In a forward position to support this right-sided attack while being ever ready to funnel back and protect his own goal if necessary.

R.C.B. In a forward position but also well-placed to protect his goal. He is in a position to cover the space behind his R.B.

L.C.B. In position to protect the whole right side of the defense.

L.B. Deeper in his own half than any of the other full-backs. He is protecting the entire defense.

R.L.M. Supporting his right and center strikers. Also ready to protect his goal.

C.L.M. Supporting the whole attack. He is in a position to help everyone.

L.L.M. In a holding position to see how the attack develops. He can go forward or backward.

R.S. Has the ball. His immediate alternatives are:
1. Attack the defense on the outside or inside.
2. Pass to his C.S. and advance into the penalty area.
3. Pass back to his R.L.M. Or he can hold the ball until either his R.L.M. or his R.B. overlap him on his right where he can pass the ball to them for it to be crossed into the penalty area.

He will select the best alternative. A good team offers alternatives.

C.S. Supporting R.S.

L.S. Staying fairly wide to stretch the opposing defense and give the attack a certain amount of width. He is not too wide and hopes his fullback will pick him up. This would leave a space for his L.L.M. to exploit.

Note that every player is in a position to be supported or to support. Support does not mean bunching. Remember, if everyone on the team supported at once, we would have "chicken soccer." As you can see from the diagram, the 10 outfield players are intelligently spread over the field. If the R.S. were to lose the ball there are seven players who are in position to funnel back and protect their goal. Should the attack break down and the ball land in the shaded area the L.C.B., R.C.B., or the R.F.B. are well positioned to advance and quickly play the ball to a teammate or into their opponent's penalty area.

This diagram on support has been included to show what can be achieved. I don't expect beginners to play this or similar systems.

A Word on Referees

At any soccer game, you can hear at least one person disagreeing with or having a go at the referee. Fair enough, it's a free country. But what would happen if there were no referees? The game would be in a bad state. In fact, there would be no game.

The referee is a necessary part of the game of soccer. He has control of players and coaches before, during, and after the game. Remember this point—it is important.

A referee is human; therefore he is fallible and liable to make mistakes. At boys' games, in particular, bear with him. In all probability, he is a young college boy who has only recently passed his referee's examination, or, possibly, he has not been a referee for more than six months. Help him; explain to your boys that the referee's word is final. Don't tongue-lash him in front of everyone if you disagree with a decision. Wait until the game is finished and ask him if he could explain the decision. This is very much a developing sport and I'm sure he'll be glad to explain his decision to you. In many cases the referee will tell you about something that you didn't see, understand or even anticipate.

In summary, be kind to referees. I wouldn't like to have their job. Would you?

Laws of the game
and Universal Guide for Referees

Issued August, 1974

AUTHORIZED BY
THE INTERNATIONAL FOOTBALL ASSOCIATION BOARD

Reprinted from the 1975-76
FIFA HANDBOOK, by kind
permission of FIFA.

NOTES

Provided the principles of these Laws be maintained, they may be modified in their application.

1. To players of school age, as follows: (a) size of playing pitch; (b) size, weight and material of ball; (c) width between the goal-posts and height of the cross-bar from the ground; (d) the duration of the periods of play.

2. For matches played by women: (a) size, weight and material of ball; (b) duration of the periods of play; (c) further modifications are only permissible with the consent of the International Football Association Board.

Laws of the Game	Decisions of the International Board

LAW I. – THE FIELD OF PLAY

The Field of Play and appurtenances shall be as shown in the following plan:

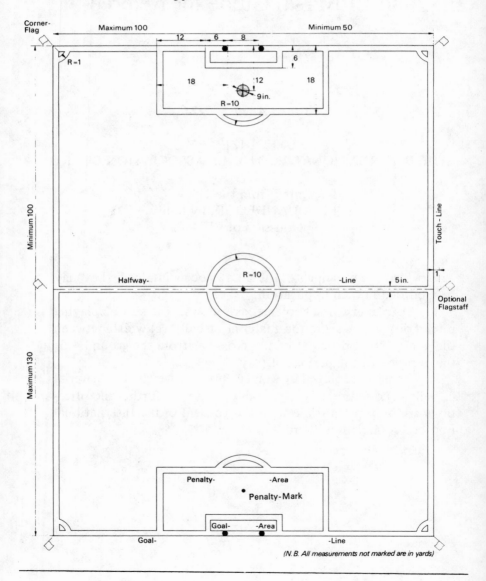

(N.B. All measurements not marked are in yards)

Laws of the Game	Decisions of the International Board

LAW I *(continued)*

(1) Dimensions. The field of play shall be rectangular, its length being not more than 130 yards nor less than 100 yards and its breadth not more than 100 yards nor less than 50 yards. (In International Matches the length shall be not more than 120 yards nor less than 110 yards and the breadth not more than 80 yards nor less than 70 yards.) The length shall in all cases exceed the breadth.

(2) Marking. The field of play shall be marked with distinctive lines, not more than 5 inches in width, not by a V-shaped rut, in accordance with the plan, the longer boundary lines being called the touch-lines and the shorter the goal-lines. A flag on a post not less than 5 ft. high and having a non-pointed top, shall be placed at each corner; a similar flag-post may be placed opposite the half-way line on each side of the field of play, not less than 1 yard outside the touch-line. A halfway-line shall be marked out across the field of play. The centre of the field of play shall be indicated by a suitable mark and a circle with a 10 yards radius shall be marked round it.

(3) The Goal-Area. At each end of the field of play two lines shall be drawn at right-angles to the goal-line, 6 yards from each goal-post. These shall extend into the field of play for a distance of 6 yards and shall be joined by a line drawn parallel with the goal-line. Each of the spaces enclosed by these lines and the goal-line shall be called a goal-area.

(4) The Penalty-Area. At each end of the field of play two lines shall be drawn at right-angles to the goal-line, 18 yards from each goal-post. These shall extend into the field of play for a distance of 18 yards and shall be joined by a line drawn parallel with the goal-line. Each of the spaces enclosed by these lines and the goal-line shall be called a penalty-area. A suitable mark shall be made within each penalty-area, 12 yards from the mid-point of the goal-line, measured along an undrawn line at right-angles thereto. These shall be the penalty-kick marks. From each penalty-kick mark an arc of a circle, having a radius of 10 yards, shall be drawn outside the penalty-area.

Decisions of the International Board

(1) In International matches the dimensions of the field of play shall be: maximum 110 x 75 metres; minimum 100 x 64 metres.

(2) National Associations must adhere strictly to these dimensions. Each National Association organising an International Match must advise the visiting Association, before the match, of the place and the dimensions of the field of play.

(3) The Board has approved this table of measurements for the Laws of the Game:

130 yards	....	120	Metres
120 yards	....	110	
110 yards	....	100	
100 yards	....	90	
80 yards	....	75	
70 yards	....	64	
50 yards	....	45	
18 yards	....	16.50	
12 yards	....	11	
10 yards	....	9.15	
8 yards	....	7.32	
6 yards	....	5.50	
1 yard	....	1	
8 feet	....	2.44	
5 feet	....	1.50	
28 inches	....	0.71	
27 inches	....	0.68	
9 inches	....	0.22	
5 inches	....	0.12	
3/4 inch	....	0.019	
1/2 inch	....	0.0127	
3/8 inch	....	0.010	
14 ounces	....	396	grams
16 ounces	....	453	grams
15 lb./sq.in.	.....	1	kg/cm^2

(4) The goal-line shall be marked the same width as the depth of the goal-posts and the cross-bar, so that the goal-line and goal-posts will conform to the same interior and exterior edges.

(5) The 6 yards (for the outline of the goal-area) and the 18 yards (for the outline of the penalty-area) which have to be measured along the goal-line, must start from the inner sides of the goal-posts.

(6) The space within the inside areas of the field of play includes the width of the lines marking these areas.

(7) All Associations shall provide standard equipment, particularly in International Matches, when the Laws of the Game must be complied with in every respect and especially with regard to the size of the ball and other equipment which must conform to the regu-

| *Laws of the Game* | *Decisions of the International Board* |

LAW 1 *(continued)*

(5) **The Corner-Area.** From each corner-flag post a quarter circle, having a radius of 1 yard, shall be drawn inside the field of play.

(6) **The Goals.** The goals shall be placed on the centre of each goal-line and shall consist of two upright posts, equidistant from the corner-flags and 8 yards apart (inside measurement), joined by a horizontal cross-bar the lower edge of which shall be 8 ft. from the ground. The width and depth of the goal-posts and the width and depth of the cross-bars shall not exceed 5 inches (12 cm). The goal-posts and the cross-bars shall have the same width.

Nets may be attached to the posts, cross-bars and ground behind the goals. They should be appropriately supported and be so placed as to allow the goal-keeper ample room.

lations. All cases of failure to provide standard equipment must be reported to F.I.F.A.

(8) In a match played under the Rules of a Competition if the cross-bar becomes displaced or broken play shall be stopped and the match abandoned unless the cross-bar has been repaired and replaced in position or a new one provided without such being a danger to the players. A rope is not considered to be a satisfactory substitute for a cross-bar.

In a Friendly Match, by mutual consent, play may be resumed without the cross-bar provided it has been removed and no longer constitutes a danger to the players. In these circumstances, a rope may be used as a substitute for a cross-bar. If a rope is not used and the ball crosses the goal-line at a point which in the opinion of the Referee is below where the cross-bar should have been he shall award a goal.

The game shall be restarted by the Referee dropping the ball at the place where it was when play was stopped.

(9) National Associations may specify such maximum and minimum dimensions for the cross-bars and goal-posts, within the limits laid down in Law I, as they consider appropriate.

(10) Goal-posts and cross-bars must be made of wood, metal or other approved material as decided from time to time by the International F.A. Board. They may be square, rectangular, round, half-round or elliptical in shape Goal-posts and cross-bars made of other materials and in other shapes are not permitted.

(11) 'Curtain-raisers' to International matches should only be played following agreement on the day of the match, and taking into account the condition of the field of play, between representatives of the two Associations and the Referee (of the International Match).

(12) National Associations, particularly in International Matches, should restrict the number of photographers and have a line marked at least 2 metres and not more than 10 metres from the goal-lines and a similar distance from the angle formed by the goal-line with the touchlines; they should prohibit photographers from passing over these lines and finally forbid the use of artifical lighting in the form of 'flashlights'.

Footnote:

Goal nets. The use of nets made of hemp, jute or nylon is permitted. The nylon strings may, however, not be thinner than those made of hemp or jute.

Laws of the Game	*Decisions of the International Board*

LAW II. – THE BALL

The ball shall be spherical; the outer casing shall be of leather or other approved materials. No material shall be used in its construction which might prove dangerous to the players.

The circumference of the ball shall not be more than 28 in. and not less than 27 in. The weight of the ball at the start of the game shall not be more than 16 oz. nor less than 14 oz. The pressure shall be equal to one atmosphere, which equals 15 lb./sq.in. (= 1 kg/cm^2) at sea level. The ball shall not be changed during the game unless authorised by the Referee.

(1) The ball used in any match shall be considered the property of the Association or Club on whose ground the match is played, and at the close of play it must be returned to the Referee.

(2) The International Board, from time to time, shall decide what constitutes approved materials. Any approved material shall be certified as such by the International Board.

(3) The Board has approved these equivalents of the weights specified in the Law: 14 to 16 ounces = 396 to 453 grammes.

(4) If the ball bursts or becomes deflated during the course of a match, the game shall be stopped and restarted by dropping the new ball at the place where the first ball became defective.

(5) If this happens during a stoppage of the game (place-kick, goal-kick, corner-kick, free-kick, penalty-kick or throw-in) the game shall be restarted accordingly.

Laws of the Game	*Decisions of the International Board*

LAW III. – NUMBER OF PLAYERS

(1) A match shall be played by two teams, each consisting of not more than eleven players, one of whom shall be the goalkeeper.

(2) Substitutes may be used in any match played under the rules of a competition, subject to the following conditions:

(a) that the authority of the international association(s) or national association(s) concerned, has been obtained,

(b) that, subject to the restriction contained in the following paragraph (c) the rules of a competition shall state how many, if any, substitutes may be used, and

(c) that a team shall not be permitted to use more than two substitutes in any match.

(3) Substitutes may be used in any other match, provided that the two teams concerned reach agreement on a maximum number, not exceeding five, and that the terms of such agreement are intimated to the Referee, before the match. If the Referee is not informed, or if the teams fail to reach agreement, no more than two substitutes shall be permitted.

(4) Any of the other players may change places with the goalkeeper, provided that the Referee is informed before the change is made, and provided also, that the change is made during a stoppage in the game.

(5) When a goalkeeper or any other player is to be replaced by a substitute, the following conditions shall be observed:

(a) the Referee shall be informed of the proposed substitution, before it is made,

(b) the substitute shall not enter the field of play until the player he is replacing has left, and then only after having received a signal from the Referee,

(c) he shall enter the field during a stoppage in the game, and at the half-way line.

Punishment:

(a) Play shall not be stopped for an infringement of paragraph 4. The players concerned shall be cautioned immediately the ball goes out of play.

(b) For any other infringement of this law, the player concerned shall be cautioned, and if the game is stopped by the Referee, to administer the caution, it shall be re-started by an indirect free-kick, to be taken by a player of the opposing team, from the place where the ball was, when play was stopped.

(1) The minimum number of players in a team is left to the discretion of National Associations.

(2) The Board is of the opinion that a match should not be considered valid if there are fewer than seven players in either of the teams.

(3) A competition may require that the referee shall be informed, before the start of the match, of the names of not more than five players, from whom the substitutes (if any) must be chosen.

(4) A player who has been ordered off before play begins may only be replaced by one of the named substitutes. The kick-off must not be delayed to allow the substitute to join his team.

A player who has been ordered off after play has started may not be replaced.

A named substitute who has been ordered off, either before or after play has started, may not be replaced (this decision only relates to players who are ordered off under Law XII. It does not apply to players who have infringed Law IV.)

(5) A player who has been replaced shall not take any further part in the game.

(6) A substitute shall be deemed to be a player and shall be subject to the authority and jurisdiction of the Referee whether called upon to play or not. For any offence committed on the field of play a substitute shall be subject to the same punishment as any other player whether called upon or not.

Laws of the Game	Decisions of the International Board

LAW IV. – PLAYERS' EQUIPMENT

(1) A player shall not wear anything which is dangerous to another player.

(2) Footwear (boots or shoes) must conform to the following standard:

(a) Bars shall be made of leather or rubber and shall be transverse and flat, not less than half an inch in width and shall extend the total width of the sole and be rounded at the corners.

(b) Studs which are independently mounted on the sole and are replaceable shall be made of leather, rubber, aluminium, plastic or similar material and shall be solid. With the exception of that part of the stud forming the base, which shall not protrude from the sole more than one quarter of an inch, studs shall be round in plan and not less than half an inch in diameter. Where studs are tapered, the minimum diameter of any section of the stud must not be less than half an inch. Where metal seating for the screw type is used, this seating must be embedded in the sole of the footwear and any atachment screw shall be part of the stud. Other than the metal seating for the screw type of stud, no metal plates even though covered with leather or rubber shall be worn, neither studs which are threaded to allow them to be screwed on to a base screw that is fixed by nails or otherwise to the soles of footwear, nor studs which, apart from the base, have any form of protruding edge rim or relief marking or ornament, should be allowed.

(c) Studs which are moulded as an integral part of the sole and are not replaceable shall be made of rubber, plastic, polyurethene or similar soft materials. Provided that there are no fewer than ten studs on the sole, they shall have a minimum diameter of three eights of an inch (10 mm.). In all other respects they shall conform to the general requirements of this Law.

(d) Combined bars and studs may be worn, provided the whole conforms to the general requirements of this Law. Neither bars nor studs on the soles shall project more than three-quarters of an inch. If nails are used they shall be driven in flush with the surface.

(3) The goalkeeper shall wear colours which distinguish him from the other players and from the referee.

(1) The usual equipment of a player is a jersey or shirt, shorts, stockings and footwear. In a match played under the rules of a competition, players need not wear boots or shoes, but shall wear jersey or shirt, shorts, or track suit or similar trousers, and stockings.

(2) The Law does not insist that boots or shoes must be worn. However, in competition matches Referees should not allow one or a few players to play without footwear when all the other players are so equipped.

(3) In International Matches, International Competitions, International Club Competitions and friendly matches between clubs of different National Associations, the Referee, prior to the start of the game, shall inspect players' boots and prevent any player whose boots do not conform to the requirements of Law IV from playing until they comply with the Law. Leagues and Competitions may include a similar provision in their rules.

(4) If the Referee finds that a player is wearing articles not permitted by the Laws and which may constitute a danger to other players, he shall order him to take them off. If he fails to carry out the Referee's instruction, the player shall not take part in the match.

(5) A player who has been prevented from taking part in the game or a player who has been sent off the field for infringing Law IV must report to the Referee during a stoppage of the game and may not enter or re-enter the field of play unless and until the Referee has satisfied himself that the player is no longer infringing Law IV.

(6) A player who has been prevented from taking part in a game or who has been sent off because of an infringement of Law IV, and who enters or re-enters the field of play to join or re-join his team, in breach of the conditions of Law XII, shall be cautioned. If the Referee stops the game to administer the caution, the game shall be restarted by an indirect free-kick, taken by a player of the opposing side, from the place where the offending player was when the Referee stopped the game.

Laws of the Game	*Decisions of the International Board*
LAW IV *(continued)* *Punishment:* For any infringement of this Law, the player at fault shall be sent off the field of play to adjust his equipment and he shall not return without first reporting to the Referee, who shall satisfy himself that the player's equipment is in order; the player shall only re-enter the game at a moment when the ball has ceased to be in play.	

Laws of the Game	Decisions of the International Board

LAW V. – REFEREES

A Referee shall be appointed to officiate in each game. His authority and the exercise of the powers granted to him by the Laws of the Game commence as soon as he enters the field of play.

His power of penalising shall extend to offences committed when play has been temporarily suspended, or when the ball is out of play. His decision on points of fact connected with the play shall be final, so far as the result of the game is concerned. He shall:

(a) Enforce the Laws.

(b) Refrain from penalising in cases where he is satisfied that, by doing so, he would be giving an advantage to the offending team.

(c) Keep a record of the game; act as timekeeper and allow the full or agreed time, adding thereto all time lost through accident or other cause.

(d) Have discretionary power to stop the game for any infringement of the Laws and to suspend or terminate the game whenever, by reason of the elements, interference by spectators, or other cause, he deems such stoppage necessary. In such a case he shall submit a detailed report to the competent authority, within the stipulated time, and in accordance with the provisions set up by the National Association under whose jurisdiction the match was played. Reports will be deemed to be made when received in the ordinary course of post.

(e) From the time he enters the field of play, caution any player guilty of misconduct or ungentlemanly behaviour and, if he persists, suspend him from further participation in the game. In such cases the Referee shall send the name of the offender to the competent authority, within the stipulated time, and in accordance with the provisions set up by the National Association under whose jurisdiction the match was played. Reports will be deemed to be made when received in the ordinary course of post.

(f) Allow no person other than the players and linesmen to enter the field of play without his permission.

(g) Stop the game if, in his opinion, a player has been seriously injured; have the player removed as soon as possible from the

Decisions of the International Board

(1) Referees in International Matches shall wear a blazer or blouse the colour of which is distinct from the colours worn by the contesting teams.

(2) Referees for International Matches will be selected from a neutral country unless the countries concerned agree to appoint their own officials.

(3) The Referee must be chosen from the official list of International Referees. This need not apply to Amateur and Youth International Matches.

(4) The Referee shall report to the appropriate authority misconduct or any misdemeanour on the part of spectators, officials, players, named substitutes or other persons which take place either on the field of play or in its vicinity at any time prior to, during, or after the match in question so that appropriate action can be taken by the Authority concerned.

(5) Linesmen are assistants of the Referee. In no case shall the Referee consider the intervention of a Linesman if he himself has seen the incident and from his position on the field, is better able to judge. With this reserve, and the Linesman neutral, the Referee can consider the intervention and if the information of the Linesman applies to that phase of the game immediately before the scoring of a goal, the Referee may act thereon and cancel the goal.

(6) The Referee, however, can only reverse his first decision so long as the game has not been restarted.

(7) If the Referee has decided to apply the advantage clause and to let the game proceed, he cannot revoke his decision if the presumed advantage has not been realised, even though he has not, by any gesture, indicated his decision. This does not exempt the offending player from being dealt with by the Referee.

(8) The Laws of the Game are intended to provide that games should be played with as little interference as possible, and in this view it is the duty of Referees to penalise only deliberate breaches of the Law. Constant whistling for trifling and doubtful breaches produces bad feeling and loss of temper on the part of the players and spoils the pleasure of spectators.

(9) By para. (d) of Law V the Referee is

Laws of the Game	*Decisions of the International Board*

LAW V *(continued)*

field of play, and immediately resume the game. If a player is slightly injured, the game shall not be stopped until the ball has ceased to be in play. A player who is able to go to the touch or goal-line for attention of any kind, shall not be treated on the field of play.

(h) Send off the field of play, any player who, in his opinion, is guilty of violent conduct, serious foul play, or the use of foul or abusive language.

(i) Signal for recommencement of the game after all stoppages.

(j) Decide that the ball provided for a match meets with the requirements of Law II.

empowered to terminate a match in the event of grave disorder, but he has no power or right to decide, in such event, that either team is disqualified and thereby the loser of the match. He must send a detailed report to the proper authority who alone has power to deal further with this matter.

(10) If a player commits two infringements of a different nature at the same time, the Referee shall punish the more serious offence.

(11) It is the duty of the Referee to act upon the information of neutral Linesmen with regard to incidents that do not come under the personal notice of the Referee.

(12) The Referee shall not allow any person to enter the field until play has stopped, and only then, if he has given him a signal to do so, nor shall he allow coaching from the boundary lines.

Laws of the Game	*Decisions of the International Board*

LAW VI. – LINESMEN

Two Linesmen shall be appointed, whose duty (subject to the decision of the Referee) shall be to indicate when the ball is out of play and which side is entitled to the corner-kick, goal-kick or throw-in. They shall also assist the Referee to control the game in accordance with the Laws. In the event of undue interference or improper conduct by a Linesman, the Referee shall dispense with his services and arrange for a substitute to be appointed. (The matter shall be reported by the Referee to the competent authority.) The Linesmen should be equipped with flags by the Club on whose ground the match is played.

(1) Linesmen, where neutral, shall draw the Referee's attention to any breach of the Laws of the Game of which they become aware if they consider that the Referee may not have seen it, but the Referee shall always be the judge of the decision to be taken.

(2) National Associations are advised to appoint official Referees of neutral nationality to act as Linesmen in International Matches.

(3) In International Matches Linesmen's flags shall be of a vivid colour, bright reds and yellows. Such flags are recommended for use in all other matches.

(4) A Linesman may be subject to disciplinary action only upon a report of the Referee for unjustified interference or insufficient assistance.

LAW VII. – DURATION OF THE GAME

The duration of the game shall be two equal periods of 45 minutes, unless otherwise mutually agreed upon, subject to the following: (a) Allowance shall be made in either period for all time lost through accident or other cause, the amount of which shall be a matter for the discretion of the Referee; (b) Time shall be extended to permit a penalty-kick being taken at or after the expiration of the normal period in either half.

At half-time the interval shall not exceed five minutes except by consent of the Referee.

(1) If a match has been stopped by the Referee, before the completion of the time specified in the rules, for any reason stated in Law V it must be replayed in full unless the rules of the competition concerned provide for the result of the match at the time of such stoppage to stand.

(2) Players have a right to an interval at half-time.

| *Laws of the Game* | *Decisions of the International Board* |

LAW VIII. – THE START OF PLAY

(a) **At the beginning of the game,** choice of ends and the kick-off shall be decided by the toss of a coin. The team winning the toss shall have the option of choice of ends or the kick-off. The Referee having given a signal, the game shall be started by a player taking a place-kick (i.e., a kick at the ball while it is stationary on the ground in the centre of the field of play) into his opponents' half of the field of play. Every player shall be in his own half of the field and every player of the team opposing that of the kicker shall remain not less than 10 yards from the ball until it is kicked-off; it shall not be deemed in play until it has travelled the distance of its own circumference. The kicker shall not play the ball a second time until it has been touched or played by another player.

(b) **After a goal has scored,** the game shall be restarted in like manner by a player of the team losing the goal.

(c) **After half-time;** when restarting after half-time, ends shall be changed and the kick-off shall be taken by a player of the opposite team to that of the player who started the game.

Punishment. For any infringement of this Law, the kick-off shall be retaken, except in the case of the kicker playing the ball again before it has been touched or played by another player; for this offence, an indirect free-kick shall be taken by a player of the opposing team from the place where the infringement occurred. A goal shall not be scored direct from a kick-off.

(d) **After any other temporary suspension;** when restarting the game after a temporary suspension of play from any cause not mentioned elsewhere in these Laws, provided that immediately prior to the suspension the ball has not passed over the touch or goal-lines, the Referee shall drop the ball at the place where it was when play was suspended and it shall be deemed in play when it has touched the ground; if, however, it goes over the touch or goal-lines after it has been dropped by the Referee, but before it is touched by a player, the Referee shall again drop it. A player shall not play the ball until it has touched the ground. If this section of the Law is not complied with the Referee shall again drop the ball.

(1) If, when the Referee drops the ball, a player infringes any of the Laws before the ball has touched the ground, the player concerned shall be cautioned or sent off the field according to the seriousness of the offence, but a free-kick cannot be awarded to the opposing team because the ball was not in play at the time of the offence. The ball shall therefore be again dropped by the Referee.

(2) Kicking-off by persons other than the players competing in a match is prohibited.

Laws of the Game	Decisions of the International Board
LAW IX. – BALL IN AND OUT OF PLAY The ball is out of play: (a) When it has wholly crossed the goal-line or touch-line, whether on the ground or in the air. (b) When the game has been stopped by the Referee. The ball is in play at all other times from the start of the match to the finish including: (a) If it rebounds from a goal-post, cross-bar or corner-flag post into the field of play. (b) If it rebounds off either the Referee or Linesmen when they are in the field of play. (c) In the event of a supposed infringement of the Laws, until a decision is given.	(1) The lines belong to the areas of which they are the boundaries. In consequence, the touch-lines and the goal-lines belong to the field of play.

Laws of the Game	*Decisions of the International Board*

LAW X. – METHOD OF SCORING

Except as otherwise provided by these Laws, a goal is scored when the whole of the ball has passed over the goal-line, between the goal-posts and under the cross-bar, provided it has not been thrown, carried or intentionally propelled by hand or arm, by a player of the attacking side, except in the case of a goalkeeper, who is within his own penalty-area.

The team scoring the greater number of goals during a game shall be the winner; if no goals, or an equal number of goals are scored, the game shall be termed a "draw".

(1) Law X defines the only method according to which a match is won or drawn; no variation whatsoever can be authorised.

(2) A goal cannot in any case be allowed if the ball has been prevented by some outside agent from passing over the goal-line. If this happens in the normal course of play, other than at the taking of a penalty-kick: the game must be stopped and restarted by the Referee dropping the ball at the place where the ball came into contact with the interference.

(3) If, when the ball is going into goal, a spectator enters the field before it passes wholly over the goal-line, and tries to prevent a score, a goal shall be allowed if the ball goes into goal unless the spectator has made contact with the ball or has interfered with play, in which case the Referee shall stop the game and restart it by dropping the ball at the place where the contact or interference occurred.

Laws of the Game	*Decisions of the International Board*

LAW XI. – OFF-SIDE

A player is off-side if he is nearer his opponents' goal-line than the ball **at the moment the ball is played unless:**

(a) He is in his own half of the field of play.

(b) There are two of his opponents nearer to their own goal-line than he is.

(c) The ball last touched an opponent or was last played by him.

(d) He receives the ball direct from a goal-kick, a corner-kick, a throw-in, or when it was dropped by the Referee.

Punishment. For an infringement of this Law, an indirect free-kick shall be taken by a player of the opposing team from the place where the infringement occurred.

A player in an off-side position shall not be penalised unless, in the opinion of the Referee, he is interfering with the play or with an opponent, or is seeking to gain an advantage by being in an offside position.

(1) Off-side shall not be judged at the moment the player in question receives the ball, but at the moment when the ball is passed to him by one of his own side. A player who is not in an off-side position when one of his colleagues passes the ball to him or takes a free-kick, does not therefore become off-side if he goes forward during the flight of the ball.

Laws of the Game	*Decisions of the International Board*

LAW XII. – FOULS AND MISCONDUCT

A player who intentionally commits any of the following nine offences:

(a) Kicks or attempts to kick an opponent;

(b) Trips an opponent, i.e., throwing or attempting to throw him by the use of the legs or by stooping in front of or behind him;

(c) Jumps at an opponent;

(d) Charges an opponent in a violent or dangerous manner;

(e) Charges an opponent from behind unless the latter be obstructing;

(f) Strikes or attempts to strike an opponent;

(g) Holds an opponent;

(h) Pushes an opponent;

(i) Handles the ball, i.e., carries, strikes or propels the ball with his hand or arm. (This does not apply to the goalkeeper within his own penalty-area);

shall be penalised by the award of a **direct free-kick** to be taken by the opposing side from the place where the offence occurred.

Should a player of the defending side intentionally commit one of the above nine offences within the penalty-area he shall be penalised by a **penalty-kick.**

A penalty-kick can be awarded irrespective of the position of the ball, if in play, at the time an offence within the penalty-area is committed.

A player committing any of the five following offences:

1. Playing in a manner considered by the Referee to be dangerous, e.g., attempting to kick the ball while held by the goalkeeper;

2. Charging fairly, i.e., with the shoulder, when the ball is not within playing distance of the players concerned and they are definitely not trying to play it;

3. When not playing the ball, intentionally obstructing an opponent, i.e., running between the opponent and the ball, or interposing the body so as to form an obstacle to an opponent;

4. Charging the goalkeeper except when he
   (a) is holding the ball;
   (b) is obstructing an opponent;

(1) If the goalkeeper either intentionally strikes an opponent by throwing the ball vigorously at him or pushes him with the ball while holding it, the Referee shall award a penalty-kick, if the offence took place within the penalty-area.

(2) If a player deliberately turns his back to an opponent when he is about to be tackled, he may be charged but not in a dangerous manner.

(3) In case of body-contact in the goal-area between an attacking player and the opposing goalkeeper not in possession of the ball, the Referee, as sole judge of intention, shall stop the game if, in his opinion, the action of the attacking player was intentional, and award an indirect free-kick.

(4) If a player leans on the shoulders of another player of his own team in order to head the ball, the Referee shall stop the game, caution the player for ungentlemanly conduct and award an indirect free-kick to the opposing side.

(5) A player's obligation when joining or rejoining his team after the start of the match to 'report to the Referee' must be interpreted as meaning 'to draw the attention of the Referee from the touch-line'. The signal from the Referee shall be made by a definite gesture which makes the player understand the he may come into the field of play; it is not necessary for the Referee to wait until the game is stopped (this does not apply in respect of an infringement of Law IV), but the Referee is the sole judge of the moment in which he gives his signal of acknowledgement.

(6) The letter and spirit of Law XII do not oblige the Referee to stop a game to administer a caution. He may, if he chooses, apply the advantage. If he does apply the advantage, he shall caution the player when play stops.

(7) If a player covers up the ball without touching it in an endeavour not to have it played by an opponent, he obstructs but does not infringe Law XII para. 3 because he is already in possession of the ball and covers it for tactical reasons whilst the ball remains within playing distance. In fact, he is actually playing the ball and does not commit an infringement; in this case, the

Laws of the Game	Decisions of the International Board

LAW XII *(continued)*

(c) has passed outside his goal-area;

5. When playing as goalkeeper,
  (a) takes more than 4 steps whilst holding, bouncing or throwing the ball in the air and catching it again without releasing it so that it is played by another player, or
  (b) indulges in tactics which, in the opinion of the Referee, are designed merely to hold up the game and thus waste time and so give an unfair advantage to his own team

shall be penalised by the award of an **indirect free-kick** to be taken by the opposing side from the place where the infringement occurred.

A player shall be **cautioned** if:

(j) he enters or re-enters the field of play to join or rejoin his team after the game has commenced, or leaves the field of play during the progress of the game (except through accident) without, in either case, first having received a signal from the Referee showing him that he may do so. If the Referee stops the game to administer the caution the game shall be restarted by an indirect free-kick taken by a player of the opposing team from the place where the offending player was when the referee stopped the game. If, however, the offending player has committed a more serious offence he shall be penalised according to that section of the law he infringed;

(k) he persistently infringes the Laws of the Game;

(l) he shows by word or action, dissent from any decision given by the Referee;

(m) he is guilty of ungentlemanly conduct.

For any of these last three offences, in addition to the caution, an **indirect free-kick** shall also be awarded to the opposing side from the place where the offence occurred unless a more serious infringement of the Laws of the Game was committed.

A player shall be **sent off** the field of play, if:

(n) in the opinion of the Referee he is guilty of violent conduct or serious foul play;

(o) he uses foul or abusive language

(p) he persists in misconduct after having received a caution.

player may be charged because he is in fact playing the ball.

(8) If a player intentionally stretches his arms to obstruct an opponent and steps from one side to the other, moving his arms up and down to delay his opponent, forcing him to change course, but does not make "bodily contact" the Referee shall caution the player for ungentlemanly conduct and award an indirect free-kick.

This applies also to players who attempt to prevent the goalkeeper from putting the ball into play in accordance with Law XII, 5 (a).

(9) If after a Referee has awarded a free-kick a player protests violently by using abusive or foul language and is sent off the field, the free-kick should not be taken until the player has left the field.

(10) Any player, whether he is within or outside the field of play, whose conduct is ungentlemanly or violent, whether or not it is directed towards an opponent, a colleague, the Referee, a linesman or other person, or who uses foul or abusive language, is guilty of an offence, and shall be dealt with according to the nature of the offence committed.

(11) If, in the opinion of the Referee a goalkeeper intentionally lies on the ball longer than is necessary, he shall be penalised for ungentlemanly conduct and
  (a) be cautioned and an indirect free-kick awarded to the opposing team;
  (b) in case of repetition of the offence, be sent off the field.

(12) The offence of spitting at opponents, officials or other persons, or similar unseemly behaviour shall be considered as violent conduct within the meaning of section (n) of Law XII.

(13) If, when a Referee is about to caution a player, and before he has done so, the player commits another offence which merits a caution, the player shall be sent off the field of play.

Laws of the Game	_Decisions of the International Board_
LAW XII _(continued)_ If play be stopped by reason of a player being ordered from the field for an offence without a separate breach of the Law having been committed, the game shall be resumed by an **indirect free-kick** awarded to the opposing side from the place where the infringement occurred.	

Laws of the Game	*Decisions of the International Board*

LAW XIII. – FREE-KICK

Free-kicks shall be classified under two headings: "Direct" (from which a goal can be scored direct against the offending side), and "Indirect" (from which a goal cannot be scored unless the ball has been played or touched by a player other than the kicker before passing through the goal).

When a player is taking a direct or an indirect free-kick inside his own penalty-area, all of the opposing players shall remain outside the area, and shall be at least ten yards from the ball whilst the kick is being taken. The ball shall be in play immediately it has travelled the distance of its own circumference and is beyond the penalty-area. The goalkeeper shall not receive the ball into his hands, in order that he may thereafter kick it into play. If the ball is not kicked direct into play, beyond the penalty-area, the kick shall be retaken.

When a player is taking a direct or an indirect free-kick outside his own penalty-area, all of the opposing players shall be at least ten yards from the ball, until it is in play, unless they are standing on their own goal-line, between the goal-posts. The ball shall be in play when it has travelled the distance of its own circumference.

If a player of the opposing side encroaches into the penalty-area, or within ten yards of the ball, as the case may be, before a free-kick is taken, the Referee shall delay the taking of the kick, until the Law is complied with.

The ball must be stationary when a free-kick is taken, and the kicker shall not play the ball a second time, until it has been touched or played by another player.

Punishment. If the kicker, after taking the free-kick, plays the ball a second time before it has been touched or played by another player an indirect free-kick shall be taken by a player of the opposing team from the spot where the infringement occurred.

(1) In order to distinguish between a direct and an indirect free-kick, the Referee, when he awards an indirect free-kick, shall indicate accordingly by raising an arm above his head. He shall keep his arm in that position until the kick has been taken.

(2) Players who do not retire to the proper distance when a free-kick is taken must be cautioned and on any repetition be ordered off. It is particularly requested of Referees that attempts to delay the taking of a free-kick by encroaching should be treated as serious misconduct.

(3) If, when a free-kick is being taken, any of the players dance about or gesticulate in a way calculated to distract their opponents, it shall be deemed ungentlemanly conduct for which the offender(s) shall be cautioned.

| *Laws of the Game* | *Decisions of the International Board* |

LAW XIV. – PENALTY-KICK

A penalty-kick shall be taken from the penalty-mark and, when it is being taken, all players with the exception of the player taking the kick, and the opposing goalkeeper, shall be within the field of play but outside the penalty-area, and at least 10 yards from the penalty-mark. The opposing goalkeeper must stand (without moving his feet) on his own goal-line, between the goalposts, until the ball is kicked. The player taking the kick must kick the ball forward; he shall not play the ball a second time until it has been touched or played by another player. The ball shall be deemed in play directly it is kicked, i.e., when it has travelled the distance of its circumference, and a goal may be scored direct from such a penalty-kick. If the ball touches the goalkeeper before passing between the posts, when a penalty-kick is being taken at or after the expiration of half-time or full-time, it does not nullify a goal. If necessary, time of play shall be extended at half-time or full-time to allow a penalty-kick to be taken.

Punishment:

For any infringement of this Law:
(a) by the defending team, the kick shall be retaken if a goal has not resulted.
(b) by the attacking team other than by the player taking the kick, if a goal is scored it shall be disallowed and the kick retaken.
(c) by the player taking the penalty-kick, committed after the ball is in play, a player of the opposing team shall take an indirect free-kick from the spot where the infringement occurred.

(1) When the Referee has awarded a penalty-kick, he shall not signal for it to be taken, until the players have taken up position in accordance with the Law.

(2) (a) If, after the kick has been taken, the ball is stopped in its course towards goal, by an outside agent, the kick shall be retaken.

(b) If, after the kick has been taken, the ball rebounds into play, from the goalkeeper, the cross-bar or a goal-post, and is then stopped in its course by an outside agent, the Referee shall stop play and restart it by dropping the ball at the place where it came into contact with the outside agent.

(3) (a) If, after having given the signal for a penalty-kick to be taken, the Referee sees that the goalkeeper is not in his right place on the goal-line, he shall, nevertheless, allow the kick to proceed. It shall be retaken, if a goal is not scored.

(b) If, after the Referee has given the signal for a penalty-kick to be taken, and before the ball has been kicked, the goalkeeper moves his feet, the Referee shall, nevertheless, allow the kick to proceed. It shall be retaken, if a goal is not scored.

(c) If, after the Referee has given the signal for a penalty-kick to be taken, and before the ball is in play, a player of the defending team encroaches into the penalty-area, or within ten yards of the penalty-mark, the Referee shall, nevertheless, allow the kick to proceed. It shall be retaken, if a goal is not scored.

The player concerned shall be cautioned.

(4) (a) If, when a penalty-kick is being taken, the player taking the kick is guilty of ungentlemanly conduct, the kick, if already taken, shall be retaken, if a goal is scored.

The player concerned shall be cautioned.

(b) If, after the referee has given the signal for a penalty-kick to be taken, and before the ball is in play, a colleague of the player taking the kick encroaches into the penalty-area or within ten yards of the penalty-mark, the Referee shall, nevertheless, allow the kick to proceed. If a goal is scored, it shall be disallowed, and the kick retaken.

The player concerned shall be cautioned.

(c) If, in the circumstances described in the foregoing paragraph, the ball rebounds into play from the goalkeeper, the cross-bar or a goal-post, the Referee in addition to

Laws of the Game	*Decisions of the International Board*
	cautioning the player, shall stop the game, and award an indirect free-kick to the opposing team, to be taken from the place where the infringement occurred. (5) (a) If, after the referee has given the signal for a penalty-kick to be taken, and before the ball is in play, the goalkeeper moves from his position on the goal-line, or moves his feet, and a colleague of the kicker encroaches into the penalty-area or within 10 yards of the penalty-mark, the kick, if taken, shall be retaken. The colleague of the kicker shall be cautioned. (b) If, after the Referee has given the signal for a penalty-kick to be taken, and before the ball is in play, a player of each team encroaches into the penalty-area, or within 10 yards of the penalty-mark, the kick, if taken, shall be retaken. The players concerned shall be cautioned. (6) When a match is extended, at half-time or full-time, to allow a penalty-kick to be taken or retaken, the extension shall last until the moment that the penalty-kick has been completed, i.e. until the Referee has decided whether or not a goal is scored. A goal is scored when the ball passes wholly over the goal-line. (a) direct from the penalty-kick, (b) having rebounded from either goal-post or the cross-bar, or (c) having touched or been played by the goalkeeper. The game shall terminate immediately the Referee has made his decision. (7) When a penalty-kick is being taken in extended time: (a) the provisions of all of the foregoing paragraphs, except paragraphs (2) (b) and (4) (c) shall apply in the usual way, and (b) in the circumstances described in paragraphs (2) (b) and (4) (c) the game shall terminate immediately the ball rebounds from the goalkeeper, the cross-bar or the goal-post.

Laws of the Game	*Decisions of the International Board*

LAW XV. – THROW-IN

When the whole of the ball passes over a touch-line, either on the ground or in the air, it shall be thrown in from the point where it crossed the line, in any direction, by a player of the team opposite to that of the player who last touched it. The thrower at the moment of delivering the ball must face the field of play and part of each foot shall be either on the touch-line or on the ground outside the touch-line. The thrower shall use both hands and shall deliver the ball from behind and over his head. The ball shall be in play immediately it enters the field of play, but the thrower shall not again play the ball until it has been touched or played by another player. A goal shall not be scored direct from a throw-in.

Punishment:

(a) If the ball is improperly thrown in the throw-in shall be taken by a player of the opposing team.

(b) If the thrower plays the ball a second time before it has been touched or played by another player, an indirect free-kick shall be taken by a player of the opposing team from the place where the infringement occurred.

(1) If a player taking a throw-in, plays the ball a second time by handling it within the field of play before it has been touched or played by another player, the Referee shall award a direct free-kick.

(2) A player taking a throw-in must face the field of play with some part of his body.

(3) If, when a throw-in is being taken, any of the opposing players dance about or gesticulate in a way calculated to distract or impede the thrower, it shall be deemed ungentlemanly conduct, for which the offender(s) shall be cautioned.

Laws of the Game	Decisions of the International Board

LAW XVI. – GOAL-KICK

When the whole of the ball passes over the goal-line excluding that portion between the goal-posts, either in the air or on the ground, having last been played by one of the attacking team, it shall be kicked direct into play beyond the penalty-area from a point within that half of the goal-area nearest to where it crossed the line, by a player of the defending team. A goalkeeper shall not receive the ball into his hands from a goal-kick in order that he may thereafter kick it into play. If the ball is not kicked beyond the penalty-area, i.e., direct into play, the kick shall be retaken. The kicker shall not play the ball a second time until it has touched – or been played by – another player. A goal shall not be scored direct from such a kick. Players of the team opposing that of the player taking the goal-kick shall remain outside the penalty-area whilst the kick is being taken.

Punishment: If a player taking a goal-kick plays the ball a second time after it has passed beyond the penalty-area, but before it has touched or been played by another player, an indirect free-kick shall be awarded to the opposing team, to be taken from the place where the infringement occurred.

(1) When a goal-kick has been taken and the player who has kicked the ball touches it again before it has left the penalty-area, the kick has not been taken in accordance with the Law and must be retaken.

Laws of the Game	*Decisions of the International Board*

LAW XVII. – CORNER-KICK

When the whole of the ball passes over the goal-line, excluding that portion between the goal-posts, either in the air or on the ground, having last been played by one of the defending team, a member of the attacking team shall take a corner-kick, i.e., the whole of the ball shall be placed within the quarter circle at the nearest corner-flag-post, which must not be moved, and it shall be kicked from that position. A goal may be scored direct from such a kick. Players of the team opposing that of the player taking the corner-kick shall not approach within 10 yards of the ball until it is in play, i.e., it has travelled the distance of its own circumference, nor shall the kicker play the ball a second time until it has been touched or played by another player.

Punishment:

(a) If the player who takes the kick plays the ball a second time before it has been touched or played by another player, the Referee shall award an indirect free-kick to the opposing team, to be taken from the place where the infringement occurred.

(b) For any other infringement the kick shall be retaken.

Diagrams
Illustrating Points
in Connection with
Off-side

NOTE

The players marked ⊗ are attacking the goal and those marked ○ are defending

Direction of movement of ball:
·••••••••••••▶

Direction of movement of player:
--------▶

Diagram 1.—OFF-SIDE

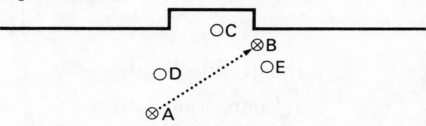

Clear pass to one of same side

A has run the ball up, and having **D** in front passes to **B**. **B** is off-side because he is in front of **A** and there are not two opponents between him and the goal-line when the ball is passed by **A**.

If **B** waits for **E** to fall back before he shoots, this will not put him on-side, because it does not alter his position with relation to **A** at the moment the ball was passed by **A**.

Diagram 2.—NOT OFF-SIDE

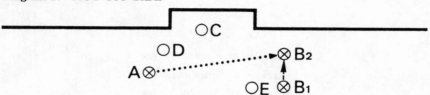

Clear pass to one of same side *(continued)*

A has run the ball up, and having **D** in front passes across the field. **B** runs from position **1** to position **2**. **B** is not off-side because at the moment the ball was passed by **A** he was not in front of the ball, and had two opponents between him and the goal-line.

Diagram 3.—OFF-SIDE

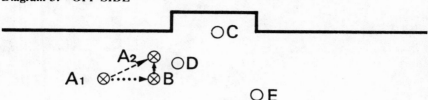

Clear pass to one of same side *(continued)*

A and **B** make a passing run up the wing. **A** passes the ball to **B** who cannot shoot because he has **D** in front. **A** then runs from position **1** to position **2** where he receives the ball from **B**. **A** is off-side because he is in front of the ball and he had not two opponents between him and the goal-line when the ball was played by **B**.

Diagram 4.—OFF-SIDE

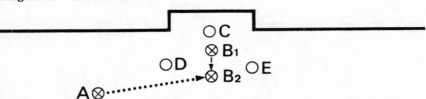

Running back for the ball

A centres the ball. **B** runs back from position **1** to position **2**, and then dribbles between **D** and **E** and scores. **B** is off-side because he is in front of the ball and he had not two opponents between him and the goal-line at the moment the ball was played by **A**.

Diagram 5.—OFF-SIDE

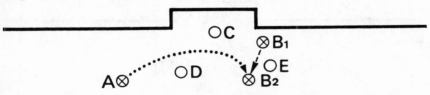

Running back for ball *(continued)*

A makes a high shot at goal, and the wind and screw carry the ball back. **B** runs from position **1** to position **2** and scores. **B** is off-side because he is in front of the ball and he had not two opponents between him and the goal-line at the moment the ball was played by **A**.

Diagram 6.—OFF-SIDE

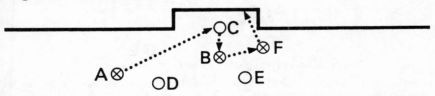

Shot at goal returned by goalkeeper **C**

A shoots at goal. The ball is played by **C** and **B** obtains possession, but slips and passes the ball to **F** who scores. **F** is off-side because he is in front of **B**, and when the ball was passed by **B** he had not two opponents between him and the goal-line.

Diagram 7.—NOT OFF-SIDE

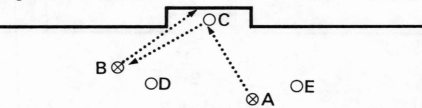

Shot at goal returned by goalkeeper *(continued)*

A shoots at goal. The ball is played out by **C** but **B** obtains possession and scores. **B** was in front of the ball and did not have two opponents between him and the goal-line when the ball was played by **A**, but he is not off-side because the ball has been last played by an opponent, **C**.

Diagram 8.—OFF-SIDE

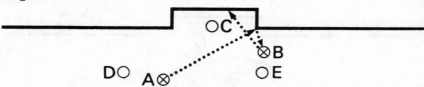

Ball rebounding from goal-posts or cross-bar

A shoots for goal and the ball rebounds from the goal-post into play. **B** secures the ball and scores. **B** is off-side because the ball is last played by **A**, a player of his own side, and when **A** played it **B** was in front of the ball and did not have two opponents between him and the goal-line.

Diagram 9.—OFF-SIDE

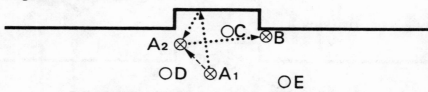

Ball rebounding from goal-posts or cross-bar *(continued)*

A shoots for goal and the ball rebounds from the cross-bar into play. **A** follows up from position **1** to position **2**, and then passes to **B** who has run up on the other side. **B** is off-side because the ball is last played by **A**, a player of his own side, and when **A** played it **B** was in front of the ball and did not have two opponents between him and the goal-line. If **A** had scored himself at the second attempt, instead of passing to **B**, it would have been a goal.

Diagram 10.—NOT OFF-SIDE

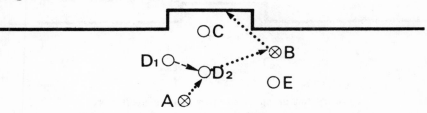

Ball touching an opponent

A shoots at goal. **D** runs from position **1** to position **2** to intercept the ball, but it glances off his foot to **B** who scores. **B** is not off-side because, although he is in front of the ball and has not two opponents between him and the goal-line the ball was last played by an opponent, **D**.

Diagram 11.—OFF-SIDE

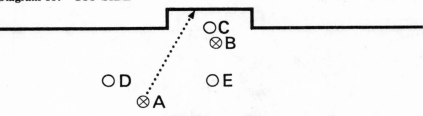

Obstructing the goalkeeper

A shoots for goal and scores. **B**, however, obstructs **C** so that he cannot get at the ball. The goal must be disallowed, because **B** is in an off-side position and may not touch the ball himself, nor in any way whatever interfere with an opponent.

Diagram 12.—OFF-SIDE

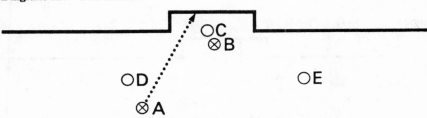

Obstructing the goalkeeper *(continued)*

A shoots for goal. **B** runs in while the ball is in transit and prevents **C** playing it properly. **B** is off-side because he is in front of **A** and has not two opponents between him and the goal-line when **A** plays the ball. When in this position **B** may not touch the ball himself, nor in any way whatever interfere with an opponent.

Diagram 13.—OFF-SIDE

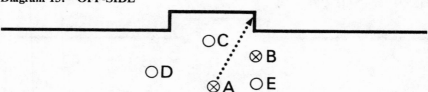

Obstructing an opponent other than the goalkeeper

A shoots for goal. **B** prevents **E** running in to intercept the ball. **B** is off-side because he is in front of **A** and has not two opponents between him and the goal-line when **A** plays the ball. When in this position **B** may not touch the ball himself, nor in any way whatever interfere with an opponent.

Diagram 14.—OFF-SIDE

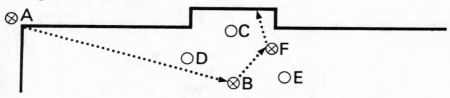

After a corner-kick

A takes a corner-kick and the ball goes to **B**. **B** shoots for goal and as the ball is passing through, **F** touches it. **F** is off-side because after the corner-kick has been taken the ball is last played by **B**, a player of his own side, and when **B** played it **F** was in front of the ball and had not two opponents between him and the goal-line.

Diagram 15.—NOT OFF-SIDE

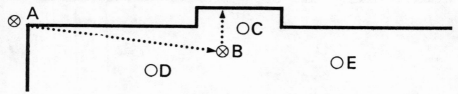

After a corner-kick *(continued)*

A takes a corner-kick and the ball goes to **B**, who puts it through goal. **B** has only one opponent between him and the goal-line, but he is not off-side because a player cannot be off-side from a corner-kick.

Diagram 16.—NOT OFF-SIDE

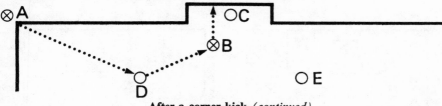

After a corner-kick *(continued)*

A takes a corner-kick and the ball glances off **D** and goes to **B**, who puts it through goal. **B** is not off-side because the ball was last played by an opponent, **D**.

Diagram 17.—OFF-SIDE

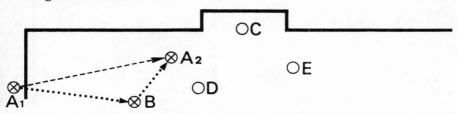

After a throw-in from the touch-line

A throws to **B** and then runs from touch-line to position **A2**. **B** passes the ball to **A** in position **2**. **A** is off-side because he is in front of the ball and has not two opponents between him and the goal-line when the ball is passed forward to him by **B**.

Diagram 18.—NOT OFF-SIDE

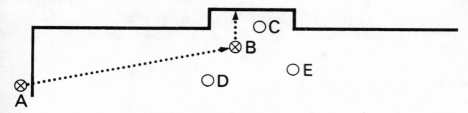

After a throw-in from the touch-line *(continued)*

A throws the ball to **B**. Although **B** is in front of the ball and has not two opponents between him and the goal line, he is not off-side because a player cannot be off-side from a throw-in.

Diagram 19.—OFF-SIDE   **Diagram 20.—NOT OFF-SIDE**

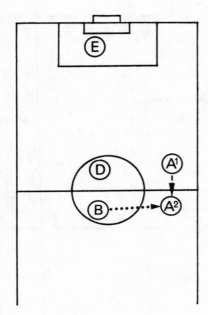

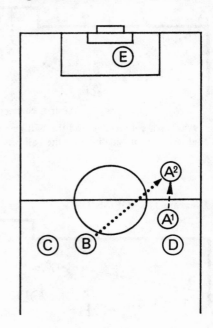

A player cannot put himself on-side by running back into his own half of the field of play

If **A** is in his opponents' half of the field of play, and is off-side in position when **B** last played the ball, he cannot put himself on-side by moving back into his own half of the field of play.

A player within his own half of the field of play is not off-side when he enters his opponents' half of the field of play

If **A** is in his own half of the field of play he is on-side, although he is in front of the ball and there are not two opponents nearer their own goal-line when **B** last played the ball. **A** is therefore not off-side when he enters his opponents' half of the field of play.

Soccer Glossary

Advantage: The clause in the Laws of the Game whereby the referee can allow the game to continue even though a foul has been committed. For instance, if the team fouled against has good attacking momentum in spite of the foul, awarding them a free kick might penalize them rather than the fouling team; it would bring their attack to a halt and give the fouling team time to regroup.

A.S.L.: American Soccer League.

Ball: Usually made of leather, the professional size five soccer ball is 27" to 28" in circumference, with a weight of 14 to 16 ounces. Boys up to age 13 normally play with a size four ball.

Banana Ball: A ball which curves as it flies, tracing out the shape of a banana.

Blocking: See "Obstruction."

Bicycle-kick: See "Scissor-kick."

Bounce-up: See "Drop-ball."

Captain: The player in charge of his team on the field.

Catenaccio: Overloading the defense. Exaggerated defense play. Italian in origin.

Center Cross: To kick the ball into the goal area or penalty area from a wide position.

Center Circle: See diagram on page 100.

Center Forward: Central forward or striker. See page 78.

Center Back or Center Fullback: One of the two central defenders usually used in modern team formations.

Center or Center kick: See "Kick-off."

Charge: A misleading term for Americans, who immediately associate it with the violence of American football. In soccer, the only legal charge is shoulder-to-shoulder contact when the ball is within playing distance.

Chesting: Controlling or stopping the ball by placing the chest in the ball's path. See "Chest Control," pages 45 and 46.

Chip: Playing the ball up in the air at a sharp angle, usually over an opponent. Very similar to a golf chip in execution.

Control: Having the ball under your command by using different parts of your body to manipulate or move it.

Corner Arc: The one-yard radius arc in all four corners of the field. Corner-kicks are taken from the corner arc.

Corner-flags: The flags atop the corner-posts.

Corner-kick: The method used for the attacking team to restart the game after the defending team has put the ball out of play over their own goal line. The kick is taken from the corner arc. The ball must be played by another player, of either team, before the kicker can play it again. A goal can be scored directly from the corner kick. See Restarts, page 76, and Set Play 2, page 91.

Corner-posts: The poles which mark the four corners of the field. (Posts and flags on the half-line are optional.) For safety they are five feet high.

Covering: Covering a colleague means supporting him when he commits himself, backing him up.

Cut-out: Intercept.

Diving: Usually this refers to a goalkeeper's throwing himself across his goal to make a save. It can also refer to a player's throwing himself at the ball to kick or head it. When diving, a player must be careful not to endanger other players.

Draw (or Tie): A game which ends with equal scores for both teams.

Dribble: Moving the ball along the ground using the insides of both feet. Controlling the ball closely. See pages 31 through 32.

Drop-ball: A method of restarting the game when a free-kick is unnecessary. The referee drops the ball at the spot where it was at the stoppage of play. He is not obliged to drop the ball between the players of opposing teams, although this is the norm. The ball must touch the ground before it can be considered in play.

End-line: See "Goal-line."

European Cup: A knock-out competition held annually to decide the top club team from each European country. The competition is played on a home and away basis. Goals scored away count double. The team having the best aggregate advances. The final is a single game; it is usually played on a neutral field.

Fake (or Feint): To move so as to wrongfoot your opponent.

Field: The playing area.

F.I.F.A.: Federation Internationale de Football Association. The world governing body of soccer.

First time ball: Passing the ball immediately, without first bringing it under control.

Flexed: Tightened.

Football: For "Football" read "Soccer" when reading all non-American and non-Canadian soccer journals. "Football" as it is known in the United States is referred to abroad as "American Football." A soccer ball overseas is called a football.

F.A.: The English Football Association.

Forward: An attacker or any player in an attacking position. When a right back advances into a forward position he is a forward and is expected to perform as one. Soccer players in today's game are increasingly called up to play in more than one position.

Formations: Various systems of arranging defenders, midfielders and attackers on the field.

4-3-3 Formation: A system of play that employs four fullbacks, three midfield players and three forwards. Goalkeepers have to be included in a team so when giving formations we always assume a goalkeeper. When reading a soccer formation start from the back. See page 83.

4-4-2-Formation: A defensive system employing four fullbacks, four midfield players and only two forwards. See page 84.

4-2-4 Formation: An attacking formation employing four full-backs, two midfield players and four forwards. See pages 82 and 83.

W-M Formation: The forerunner of today's modern systems of play. See page 81.

Free-kicks: A direct free-kick is awarded for a foul. The kick is taken from the spot where the foul occurred (excepting penalties—see Laws XII and XIV for clarification.) A goal can be scored directly from this kick. Defenders must stand 10 yards from the ball until it is played. The ball must be played by another player, or either team, before the kicker can play it again. See pages 114 and 118.

An Indirect free-kick is awarded for a foul. Once again the kick is taken from the spot where the foul occurred. A goal *cannot* be scored directly from an indirect free-kick; the ball has to touch another player first—of either team. Defenders, whenever possible (see Law XIII), must stand 10 yards from the ball until it is played. A referee signals an indirect free-kick by another player, of either team, before the kicker plays again.

Foul: An act against the laws of the game. An infringement or attempted infringement of these laws. The referee can award a direct or indirect free-kick when a foul occurs while also having the power to take disiplinary action if he sees fit. He can caution players or eject them.

Funnel-back: Retreating to defend one's goal.

Goalkeeper (or Goal-tender): The only player on a team allowed to handle the ball. This he can do only with the confines of his own penalty area. He is allowed outside of his penalty area but is then subject to the same rules as the other outfield players. See pages 53 through 55.

Goal-kick: A kick awarded to the defending team when the attacking team has played the ball over the defenders' goalline but not through their goal. A goal-kick must travel outside of the penalty area before it can be played. The ball must be played by another player, of either side, before the kicker can play it again. See page 121. Restarts page 77 and Set Play No. 2 page 91.

Goal-line: The back-line or end-line between the corner flags on which the goal lies. See page 100.

Goal-net: The net covering the back of the goal.

Give and Go: Passing to a colleague, then moving into open space to receive the return pass.

Goals: The structures at either end of the field, 8 ft. high and 8 yds. wide and standing on the goal-lines. See goal-posts. Also, the object of the game, the team with the most goals at the end of the game being the winner. A goal is scored when the ball is legitimately played between the goal-posts, underneath the crossbar and over the goal line.

Goal area: Often referred to as the goal-keeper's box. The goal area extends into the field of play in front of the goal measuring 6 yds. x 20 yds. (See page 100.)

Goal-posts: The two uprights (8 ft. high) that support the crossbar (8 yds. long). The posts and crossbar comprise each goal one at each end of the field.

Halfback: Linkman. See page 78.

Half-time: The interval between the two 45 minute periods of play.

Half-Volley: Playing the ball as it strikes the ground. As in tennis.

Handball: Intentionally playing the ball with the hands or arms. In such cases the referee can award a direct free kick. A defending player handling in his own penalty area would give away a penalty. The goalkeeper is the obvious exception to this rule, but only inside his penalty area. Handball applies from the top of the shoulders down to the finger tips.

Half-way Line: The line that cuts the field in two, parallel to the goal-lines.

Hat-trick: A British term meaning three of anything. In soccer, three goals in one game.

Heading: Unique to soccer. A method of controlling, passing and scoring whereby the forehead meets the ball. See pages 26 through 28.

Heeling (Back Heeling): Playing the ball by using the heel. Usually done while dribbling. This is a highly developed skill which, when used effectively, can change the play dramatically.

Indoor Soccer: Playing soccer indoors, often in an ice hocky rink covered with artificial turf, with modifications on the number of players per team, the size of the goal and the number of substitutions, etc. Playing off the boards is the biggest difference from playing outdoor soccer.

Instep: The top of the foot, where the shoes are laced. See page 14.

Interception: Legally cutting out or interfering with a play of the opposition. See Reading the Game.

International: Read "All Star" for "International."

Juggling: Keeping the ball in the air by constantly touching it with various parts of the body except the hands. Practicing juggling improves one's feel for the ball.

Kick-off (or Center): The kick which starts the game or restarts it after a goal. The ball must travel forward the distance of its circumference before it can be played or deemed to be in play. See Restarts, pages 76 and 110. The ball must be played another player, of either team, before the kicker can play it again.

Kill the ball: To trap the ball. To stop the ball's motion. See "Trap."

Linesmen: Two officials who assist the referee, one on either side of the field, each covering one half. They communicate with the central official by the use of flags.

Linkmen: Midfield players who join attack with defense. The engine-room of the team. Also referred to as halfbacks.

Loft or lob: A high arching, gentle kick or head, or, in the case of the suggested practices in this book, a throw.

Marking: For "Marking," read "Guarding."

Match: Game.

N.A.S.L.: North American Soccer League.

Nations Cup: Contested every four years by European All-star teams.

N.C.A.A.: National Collegiate Athletic Association. America's governing body of collegiate sports.

Obstruction: Illegally stepping in the path of an opponent to impede his progress.

Offside: Applies when the ball is passed to a player by a colleague, the player receiving the ball being in his opponent's half of the field with less than two opponents between him and his opponent's goal-line when the ball was last played. Law XI (Read offside section for exceptions.) Read Law XI thoroughly. See offside section, pages 123 through 130, also Law XI on page) 113.

Overlap: A player joining with his attack by running down the touchline past a forward player.

Own-goal: Scoring a goal for the other team.

Overhead Kick: Kicking the ball back over one's head.

Pace: The speed on the ball. To take the pace off of a ball means to slow it down, to take the power out of it.

Pass: Playing the ball from one player to another.

Penalty Arc: At all direct free-kicks the opposition must stand 10 yards from the kicker. This was difficult to gauge on a penalty as the penalty spot is 12 yards from the goal-line, only six yards from the edge of the penalty area. To enforce the 10-yard rule, an arc of 10 yards radius is drawn from the penalty spot.

Penalty Area (or Penalty box): Measuring 18 x 44 yards, the penalty-area extends into the field of play containing the goal and the goal area. A direct free-kick given against the defending team for an infringement inside the penalty area is automatically a penalty. Penalty kicks can only be awarded for infringements which occur inside the penalty area. The most common cause of penalties is the handball. See pages 76, 78, 95, and 118.

Penalty-kick: A direct kick taken by the team offended against from in front of the goal, 12 yards out from the center of the goal-line. All defenders and attackers must stand inside the field of play but outside of the penalty-area. Only the goalkeeper and the kicker are allowed inside the penalty area when the kick is being taken. The goalkeeper must stand on his goal-line and cannot move his feet until the ball has been kicked. This situation very much favors the kicker although he is only allowed one touch of the ball.

There is much confusion between the terms "penalty" and "free-kick." Both are awarded for fouls. Penalties are awarded for any foul by the defending team, inside its penalty area, which is penalized by a direct free kick. This is the only time the word "penalty" is used correctly. Free kicks outside of the penalty area cannot be called penalties. They are called "free-kicks" whether "direct" or "indirect." (Indirect free-kicks can be awarded inside the penalty area.)

Penalty Spot: The spot 12 yards from the goal-line where penalty kicks are taken from. See page 100.

Pick-up: For "Pick-up" read "Guard."

Pitch: The playing area. The field of play.

Place-kick: A kick which has been awarded or won (i.e., a free-kick or corner-kick), whereby the ball is placed on the ground prior to kicking.

Play (or Playing): Playing the ball means passing.

Quarter Circle (Quarter Arc): Where a corner-kick is taken from. See Corner Arc.

Reading the Game: Understanding the game's development. This enables a team to anticipate opponents' moves and at the same time to put their own moves into action.

Referee: The chief official. He has control of the game before, during and after play. His word is law. The referee has the further power of cautioning or ejecting players if he deems it necessary. He is assisted by two linesmen.

Save: To prevent a goal or defuse a dangerous situation.

Scissor-kick: Kicking the ball in the air when both legs are in the air and one leg crosses the other in a scissors motion.

Screen (Shield): Keeping possession of the ball by placing the body between the ball and an opponent when the ball is within playing distance.

Shin-guards: Protective pads or guards for the shins. A very sensible precaution.

Side: Team.

Sideline: The lines which connect the corners of either side of the field. They could just as well be called the throw-in lines as all throw-ins are taken from these lines. Also known as touch-lines. See page 100.

Striker: Modern term for forward.

Support: See pages 95 through 97.

Sweeper: A defender who backs up his fellow defensemen.

Sometimes positioned in front of but more usually behind the back four.

Tackle: Attempting to win the ball from an opponent when both players are playing the ball with their feet. See pages 48 through 50.

Tactics: The methods by which a team plays—using their abilities to the full and hiding their limitations.

Team: In soccer, 11 players, one of whom must be the goalkeeper, make up a team.

Thirty-five-yard Line: In the NASL, offsides apply only between the 35-yard lines and the goal-lines, not from the half-way lines and the goal-lines.

Through-pass: A pass which attempts to by-pass a defensive line-up by going through or over defenders enabling attacking players to run onto the ball.

Throw-in: The method of restarting the game when a ball has gone out of bounds over the sidelines. A goal cannot be scored directly from a throw-in. The ball must be played by another player, of either team, before the thrower can play it again.

Touch-line: See Sideline.

Transfer: A trade of a player from one team to another.

Transfer Fee: The sum one club pays to another for a player's services.

Trap: Controlling the ball by stopping it with any part of the body except the arms and hands.

U.S.S.F.: United States Soccer Federation. This body governs soccer in the United States.

Volley: Kicking the ball when it is in the air.

Wall: A defensive line-up which aids the goalkeeper. See

Wall Pass: Passing the ball to a colleague and running for a first-time pass into a space. The same effect as if the ball was hit off a wall. Almost identical to a " Give and Go. "

Wing: See Winger. Also refers to the areas on the side of the field where a winger normally plays.

Winger: One of two forwards who flank the center forward. Modern systems sometimes use only one winger while others do not use them at all.

Wing-half: In the W-M formation the wing halves are employed beside the center half, one on his right and one on his left.

World Cup: The international championship of the world, contested every four years. The best teams in the world compete to decide the championship. Preliminaries take two years. The finals usually take three weeks. Each final is held in a different country. In 1974, an estimated 800 million people watched the championship game live on TV. In 1982, over one billion fans watched the finals. The World Cup is a test of stamina and organization as well as ability and skill.

Past, Present, and Future

Kicking comes naturally. Whether we kick a tin can or a soccer ball matters little; in both cases, it seems to satisfy a basic desire. No one knows when man first began to play games based on kicking, but they seem to have been common all over the world. We have records of games akin to soccer being played in ancient China and Egypt, in Greece and Rome, and on up to more recent times.

The English monarchs, including King Edward III, King Richard II, King Henry IV, and Queen Elizabeth I, banned soccer because it kept the yeoman away from archery practice and was thus threatening the security of the realm. The game persisted, however, growing into massive contests in which whole villages played against each other. The object was to get the blown-up bladder of an animal into the opposing village. As far as we know, any means were legal. Each team consisted of hundreds of men and games were extremely rough.

By the early 1800s, soccer had progressed from this primitive rough and tumble. Although the rules varied considerably from club to club, a certain amount of uniformity appeared. But the game remained rough. A Frenchman watching the game couldn't believe it was being played for fun. He remarked, "If this is the way Englishmen play, I certainly don't want to see them fighting."

In 1823, a football game at Rugby School was in progress when William Webb Ellis picked up the ball and ran with it. This act split football into two games, "Association Football" (soccer) and "Rugby Football" (rugby is the daddy of American football).

In 1863, laws were drawn up in London for "Association Football." Even so the game was still a long way from the version we play today. Slowly the game and the laws evolved. It was only in 1883, for instance, that the first wooden crossbar appeared. Today, soccer is played by the same laws the world-over.

Soccer in the United States is neither a new nor a foreign sport. This misconception can now be laid to rest. The fact is, soccer has been here a long time, but it's been played almost exclusively by Ivy League colleges and ethnic groups in the backwaters of the American sports scene. This state of affairs is changing rapidly: soccer is now entering the sports mainstream.

Major Milestones

1869—The first intercollegiate game is played between Rutgers and Princeton.

1884—The US Soccer Football Association is formed.

1900—The US Intercollegiate Soccer Association is formed.

1913—The US Soccer Football Association joins FIFA.

1930—The US reaches semi-finals of first World Cup in Uruguay.

1934—The US enters the World Cup in Italy. In first round it beats Mexico, 4-0. Buff Donelli scored all four goals.

1950—The US enters the World Cup in Brazil and scores one of sport's greatest upsets by beating England, 1-0.

1959—The NCAA sponsors the first National Collegiate Championship tournament. St. Louis University wins.

1966—Major league professional soccer comes to the US.

1972—A US soccer team qualifies for the Olympics for the first time.

1973—The US beats Poland 1-0, playing against the same team that finished third in 1974 World Cup.

This is the record of a country that has, up to now, taken soccer lightly. What can we achieve when we take it seriously? Everything!

So much for the past. What of the future? I think the future of US soccer looks very, very good. I base this not only on my own observations but also on reports from all over the country. American children are strong, fit, agile, easy to teach, willing to learn, and rapidly gaining surprisingly good soccer skills.

Above all, they have tremendous desire. When compared with their soccer-playing counterparts in South America and Europe they are not far behind. The gap is closing rapidly. When these young players become as skillful as their foreign counterparts, the US will stand an excellent chance of dominating world soccer.

Soccer at the high school level continues to improve as does college soccer where each year the players increase in knowledge and skills. This is constantly forcing up standards. In a few years, US soccer will produce more than just one or two outstanding players per year in the college draft. The tip of the iceberg is only just beginning to appear. The game at the high school and college level is healthy.

Over the last few years, US soccer has developed steadily in the professional ranks too. There are now two main leagues, the A.S.L. and the N.A.S.L. Although it operates only in the northeast, the A.S.L. appears to be holding its own. Great progress is being made by the N.A.S.L., which has teams coast to coast as well as in Canada. The N.A.S.L. now appears to be lining up to its unwritten motto of "going big time."

1972—The N.A.S.L. holds its first college draft.

1973—The N.A.S.L. expands to nine teams.

1974—The N.A.S.L. expands to 15 teams.

1974—The N.A.S.L. Championship game is televised live on national TV.

1974—The inauguration of "Rio Grande Plate"—an annual home and away competition played between the US and Mexico. Although this competition is not entirely run by the N.A.S.L., it is supported by the league.

1975—The N.A.S.L. holds the first indoor tournament, which is televised twice at peak viewing times.

1975—The N.A.S.L. expands to 20 teams.

1975—The N.A.S.L., for the first time, sets the championship game prior to season play.

1977—An N.A.S.L. playoff game in the Giants Stadium at New York drew over 77,000 spectators.

1984—One third of the paying attendance at the Summer Olympics Games was for soccer.

The foundations for the future are fast being laid. The game at the pro level is healthy.

US soccer has a secret weapon: the fairer sex. Girls' leagues are sprouting all over the country. Women provide around 40% of the fan support for the N.A.S.L. They are active in organizing and coaching in the boys' leagues and also in forming their own leagues. And who does the majority of the calling and running children to practice and games? The women of this country. I believe that women will make a major contribution to US soccer.

If the US has the faith and the foresight to use its facilities for the development of soccer in this country, the game will benefit immeasurably. If this faith and foresight is backed by money, sensibly spent, then there is nothing that cannot be achieved.

I feel that in 10 years soccer will be one of America's biggest sports. In 20 years I believe it will be the biggest. I further believe that in 20 years America will be one of the strongest soccer nations in the world, if not the strongest. I make the above claims because I see improvements everywhere; in the administration and educational fields, as well as in officiating, and, most important, in playing ability.

In short, US soccer is emerging from its dark age as Americans begin to identify with the sport. Much remains to be done, but the barriers are crumbling at an ever-increasing rate. Great strides have been made, but the main task is still ahead. We must not rest on our laurels.

If I were asked to describe my feelings about the future of US soccer my reply would be "Positive." I'm positive *the game* has a great future.

Here's to soccer in the US. Let's all work for it's betterment.

Look for these books of interest from Runner's World and Collier Books

The Runner's World Knee Book

The Runner's World Training Diary

Running After Forty

Dance Aerobics

The Competitive Runner's Training Book

Cures for Common Running Injuries

Run Farther, Run Faster

Running to the Top

The Triathlon Training Book

The Runner's World Weight Control Book

Building Bicycle Wheels

Beginner's Racquetball

Fundamentals of Bodybuilding

Running for Women

Practical Soccer Tactics

The Basic Soccer Guide